"THE SERVANT IN THE HOUSE" PLEASES ST. PAUL

The most noteworthy attraction that has been on the boards of the Metropolitan this season and one of the most remarkable plays ever produced in an American theater opened last night for a three nights' stand. "The Servant in the House" by Charles Rann Kennedy is the piece, one that enjoyed an instantaneous and tremendous success in New York; a fact that called forth the remark from a Western critic that for once Gotham was pleased to approve of something that is really worth while.

"The Servant in the House" has a thing that a great drama must have and that is a noble aim. It is that of presenting in a form that will impress both the heart and mind of the present generation, the spirit of the Christ as it may appear in modern life. Its most marked feature is an audacious portrayal of the character of Jesus Christ disguised as an Indian butler. The literary finish of the play is quite as noteworthy as the reverent, compelling vitality of the theme and action themselves—though it is essentially a play to be acted, being chiseled along the severely classic lines of the works of Sophocles and Ibsen. It rather out-Greeks either of them, however, in its unities of time and place of action. The four acts of the drama, which revolutionizes several human lives, take place between the breakfast hour and noon; and the scene is unchanged throughout, being the breakfast room in the vicarage.

Very briefly the story is that of three brothers, one a successful East Indian bishop, one a rising young vicar in an English church and the third a drunkard and an outcast, by occupation a cleaner of drains. The bishop is Joshua, who masquerades as "Manson," a butler, but literally the Son of Man; the vicar is William, the husband of Martha, who goes by the name of Auntie, and the outcast is Robert, the father of Mary, the little child who leads them. William has risen to his prominence in the church over the body of Robert, who scrimped and benighted himself to educate the youngest brother, and is repaid by William and Auntie adopting Mary upon the death of her mother, while Robert himself is an unrecognized member of the family. As he says: "They's a lot o' brothers about as ye' don't know on't. Eh, what?" Mary is kept in ignorance of her father until the play opens, when she is about fifteen years old.

The piece opens with signs of stress and struggle written upon the faces of two of the characters, the vicar, who tries to throw off the schackles

which they [...]

The recognition and reconciliation of the three brothers takes place when Robert returns from investigating the drain under the church and finds the fault to be a grave. The act of purifying it may sacrifice a man's life, but he decides to sacrifice himself, understanding the nobility in the work, and cheerfully offering up himself that the people may go on as before—praying and singing in the church above. The suggestion of Christ is carried with reverence and good taste.

The inevitable universal brotherhood of man and the fact that the hunger for that brotherhood is at the bottom of the unrest in the modern world are the underlying thought of the play, and it is a wonderful lesson and an inspiration. Manson's scheme in coming to untangle the difficulties of a family is, as he tells Mary, "the spinning of a fairy tale," and the very delightful fact that the piece makes clear is that "anything will come true, if you only wish hard enough." It is essentially a drama of an idea, and its appeal is dramatic rather than theatrical; there is practically no scenery—it depends for its interest mainly on the clash of character on character in the working out of a struggle of human souls. There are no stage devices and alluring lights; and it might be played as successfully without any scenery at all.

It is quite possible that a company of such uniform excellence and brilliance has never been heard in St. Paul, and it has not been heralded as an "all-star" cast either.

The cast includes seven persons. George W. Wilson, achieves a character study in the part of the Bishop of Lancashire, the symbol of the "rottenness" in the church, which is unquestionably the highest pinnacle he has attained in his long career of character successes. Wilfred Rogers plays the vicar with force and conviction. Miss Lizzie Hudson Collier as "Auntie," gets into the part with complete spontaneity, completely rounding out one's preconceived idea of the character. Miss Gladys Wynnne, the ingenue, is a consummate little actress in that she seems to live, and not act her lines and business.

Henry Dornton is a clever page boy. Creston Clarke, as Manson, has manifest-

DRAMATIC

METROPOLITAN.

Charles Rann Kennedy's much discussed play "The Servant in the House" made its first Minneapolis appearance last evening at the Metropolitan opera house, before an audience whose size and quality indicated the deep and widespread interest that the symbolical masterpiece has aroused among reading and thinking people.

"The Servant in the House."

"The Servant in the House" has been repeatedly called "the greatest play of the last decade." This superlative phrase naturally attracts interested attention and arouses anticipation; but, after seeing the play itself, the description seems careless and inefficient. To call "The Servant in the House" the greatest play of the last decade places it, by implication, in a class where it does not belong. In construction, sustained interest, purity and simple strength of language, progressive intensity of narrative, finished workmanship and all the rest of the fundamentals it may rightly challenge comparison fearlessly; for it stands all these tests very well, though not well enough to be called, from this ordinary standard, "the greatest play of the last decade."

The most wonderful thing that Mr. Kennedy has accomplished in writing his wonderful play, is to produce a dramatic work that is in a class by itself. It combines with fine dramaturgy the atmosphere of the old morality play, the imagery of a supernatural allegory, and a subtlety of symbolism that fill the incidents of a crucial day in the family life of an English vicarage with undermeanings as deep as religion or eternity itself. Its uniqueness in the dramatic field is due largely to the incomparable interweaving of its duality. To the superficial theater-goer it offers sustained amusement and thrill of the kinds he loves best, not unmixed with amusement and unfolding a story that, though it must puzzle him at times, is of engrossing interest. To the analyst, thinker and philosopher it reveals many facets that shine from the jewel of all the combined philosophies of the world—and of other worlds, too, perhaps—the jewel of perfect love and universal brotherhood. "The Servant in the House" is a powerful preachment; it makes you think, whether you are a saint or a sinner. But it is a preachment with but few and scattered moments of depression or heaviness, and free, while you are hearing it at least, of any direct and uncomfortable accusation against yourself.

These accusations may strike home after you have left the playhouse, and perhaps not until the play has been seen a second or even a third time, for none of us can claim, even in our occasional flashes of honesty with ourselves, to have come fully into the universal perfection of human brotherhood that would solve all the problems of earth and make heaven almost needless. Of no other dramatic preachment can all this be truthfully said, whether it lie anywhere between a medieval morality play and a Henry Arthur Jones problem-satire, or in the region occupied by George Bernard Shaw, whose undoubted power is so warped by whimsicality that his audience rarely knows when he is in earnest.

There is no doubt about the earnestness of "The Servant in the House." From the central figure, Manson, springs the spirit that permeates the play, rising from it like a perfume that clings to every hearer after the curtain has fallen. This figure, the least subtly symbolical and ethical of any in the play, is daringly that of the Christ spirit and teachings in visible and recognizable form; so daringly that its presence, face, voice and gestures seem ever on the verge of sacrilege, without ever crossing it. He comes, the real brother of a vicar of England, in the semblance of a butler to the vicarage, where his great work of purging the house of Mammon and bringing to it the benison of truth and love must be done. This work he emphasizes by service. After he has done his work; when the "money changer" has been scourged from the temple" and when the parted family group stand in attitudes of affection he reveals himself quietly as he lays the cloth upon the dining table. His brother, still puzzled and half doubting, exclaims:

"In God's Name, who are you?"

And Manson replies, as the final curtain slowly falls:

"In God's Name, your brother."

All the philosophies of all the ages; all the central truths of all the religions, are summed up in that final answer:

"In God's Name, your brother."

The gratitude of the many thousands all over the country who will have their first opportunity this winter of seeing "The Servant in the House" is due to Henry Miller for the high standard he has maintained after taking the original company out of the play and filling their places for the road. The present company compares favorably at all points with that headed by Walter Hampden, Tyrone Power and Edith Wynne Matthison, whose admirable interpretation they follow closely in every detail. If there be an impression that the performance is not quite so perfect as that of the former company, it is so slight that it remains only an impression, too fleeting and hidden to be analyzed in detail.

The role of Manson (the Bishop of Benares) is played with deep sincerity and reverence for its sacred source by Creston Clarke, who surmounts its unprecedented difficulties of earnest finesse with perfect and impressive result. His watchful, earnest eyes, his gentle, resonant voice, his gestures so suggestive of familiar pictures of the Man of Galilee, accentuate the force of the character's physical and mental resemblances.

Clay Clement plays the subtly symbolical role of the drain-man, and plays it magnificently. Those who saw Tyrone Power in this wonderful role will remember his impersonation as one of the most perfect bits of dramatic realism possible, but Mr. Clement's finely finished and intelligent acting counts even in conflict with his memory. He very wisely takes Mr. Power's conception as a model, and strikes truly the same certain keynote of combined contrast and accordance that makes the rough figure of the drain-man so powerful a unit in both the superficial and the deeper action of the dual drama. In the beautiful scene with Mary, which is the dramatic gem of the performance, his strong, feeling work is beyond criticism. George W. Wilson, the eminent character actor, appears as James Ponsonby Makeshyfte, D. D., the Lord Bishop of Lancashire, symbolically representative of expediency and selfishness in the church and in the world, of those who "have eyes but they see not and ears but they hear not." Mr. Wilson's embodiment of the role is a marvel of makeup and of acting, its comedy a trifle too broad, perhaps, for its more serious significances, but cast in the right mold and tremendously effective. Lizzie Hudson Collier has Miss Matthison's former part of the vicar's wife, a role deceptively easy in that it requires only naturalness and sincerity, which, when attained as perfectly as Miss Collier attains them, prove the priceless and rare possession of the art that conceals art. Gwladys Wynne is the only member of the former company still seen in the play. She gives to the girlish role of Mary a truly appellant innocence and trustful frankness, remindful of the lines from Longfellow's "Maidenhood":

"Standing with reluctant feet,
Where the brook and river meet;
Womanhood, and childhood fleet."

Wilfred Rogers plays the rector, struggling to enter the region of truth he sees so clearly before him, very well and impressively, and Henry Dornton is excellent as the page, who cannot understand what it is all about.

There being no change of scenery, the curtain remains down but a brief moment between most of the so-called acts, and the impression of continuity is ingeniously preserved by having the characters of the play when it rises, still standing in the positions they occupied when it fell. Thus the fall and rise of the curtain is hardly more of an interruption than the turning of a page in a book.

Only three musical numbers are played during the longer intervals of the action, for all are not of the same brevity, and these were wisely selected to be used at all performances of the play, instead of being left to the random choice of scattered local musical directors. They are all from Beethoven, the first being the Egmont overture, the second the first movement of the Sonata in C sharp minor, generally known as the "Moonlight Sonata," and the third the Adagio from the "Sonata Pathetique."

CARYL B. STORRS.

MANSON

THE
SERVANT
IN THE HOUSE

BY
CHARLES RANN KENNEDY

ILLUSTRATED WITH PORTRAITS OF
THE CHARACTERS IN THE PLAY

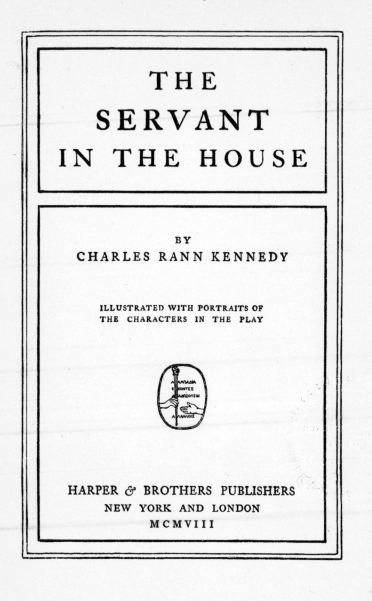

HARPER & BROTHERS PUBLISHERS
NEW YORK AND LONDON
MCMVIII

TO

WALTER HAMPDEN

" There's a lot o' brothers
knockin' abaht as people
don't know on, eh what ?
See wot I mean ?"

"He that saith he is in the light, and hateth his brother, is in darkness even until now. He that loveth his brother abideth in the light, and there is none occasion of stumbling in him. But he that hateth his brother is in darkness, and walketh in darkness and knoweth not whither he goeth, because that darkness hath blinded his eyes. . . . If a man say, I love God, and hateth his brother, he is a liar: for he that loveth not his brother whom he hath seen, how can he love God whom he hath not seen?"

—I. JOHN, ii. 9–11 ; iv. 20.

"The hunger for brotherhood is at the bottom of the unrest of the modern civilized world."

—GEORGE FREDERICK WATTS.

ORIGINAL CAST OF CHARACTERS

IN

THE SERVANT IN THE HOUSE

BY

CHARLES RANN KENNEDY

AS PRESENTED BY

THE HENRY MILLER ASSOCIATE PLAYERS

AT

THE SAVOY THEATRE, NEW YORK

ON MONDAY, MARCH 23, 1908

A PLAY OF THE PRESENT DAY, IN FIVE ACTS, SCENE INDIVIDABLE
SETTING FORTH THE STORY OF ONE MORNING IN THE EARLY SPRING

PERSONS IN THE PLAY

JAMES PONSONBY MAKESHYFTE, D.D., The Most Reverend,
The Lord Bishop of Lancashire . . . Mr. ARTHUR LEWIS

THE REVEREND WILLIAM SMYTHE, Vicar,
Mr. CHARLES DALTON

AUNTIE, the Vicar's Wife . Miss EDITH WYNNE MATTHISON

MARY, their niece . . . . Miss MABEL MOORE

MR. ROBERT SMITH, a gentleman of necessary occupation,
Mr. TYRONE POWER

ROGERS, a page-boy . . . . . . Mr. GALWEY HERBERT

MANSON, a butler . . . . . . Mr. WALTER HAMPDEN

Time—An early morning in Spring.

Place—An English country vicarage.

ILLUSTRATIONS

*The portraits of the characters in the play
have been reproduced from photographs
made for the book by Miss Alice Boughton.*

CHARACTERS REPRESENTED

JAMES PONSONBY MAKESHYFTE, D.D.
The Most Reverend the Lord Bishop of Lancashire

THE REVEREND WILLIAM SMYTHE
The Vicar

AUNTIE
The Vicar's Wife

MARY
Their niece

MR. ROBERT SMITH
A gentleman of necessary occupation

ROGERS
A page-boy

MANSON
A butler

TIME: Now
PLACE: Here

THE SCENE

The scene, which remains unchanged throughout the play, is a room in the vicarage. Jacobean in character, its oak-panelling and beamed-ceiling, together with some fine pieces of antique furniture, lend it an air of historical interest, whilst in all other respects it speaks of solid comfort, refinement, and unostentatious elegance. Evidently the room of a rich man, who has, however, apparently come to some compromise on the difficult question of his entrance into the Kingdom of Heaven; for the panelled walls possess, among other decorations, a richly ornamented crucifix, a Virgin and Child by an old master, certain saints in ecstasy, and a really remarkable modern oil-painting of the Divine Author of our religion.

The main door of the room is at the back of the stage, somewhere towards the middle; it opens upon a hall, at the further side of which one may perceive, through the open door of another room, a goodly collection of well-bound and learned-looking volumes—the vicar's library. At the present moment these tomes of wisdom are inaccessible, as the library door is blocked up with unsightly mounds of earth, sewer-pipes, and certain workmen's implements. The fact is, the vicarage has been greatly dis-

[13]

turbed of late, owing to a defect in the drainage—an unsavory circumstance which receives further and regretful explication in the play itself.

Returning, then, to the room, one may see, in addition to the main door described above, another door, to the right of stage, and near to the audience. The curious may be glad to learn that this leads into a drawing-room, and incidentally affords one more means of communication with the house. Another exit is provided on the opposite side of the stage [left], where a couple of lofty French windows lead out into the garden. Above the drawing-room door is a fine old Jacobean mantel-piece: a fire burns brightly in the grate. To the left of the main door at the back is a long, low, mullioned window, through which one may see a blue sky, a thatched top or two of cottages, and the gray old tower of the church. Through the French windows are seen a gravel-walk, a lawn, trees, and a sun-dial.

Of the essential furniture of the scene, there may be mentioned: sideboard to right of main door; table, right-centre of stage, with chairs; arm-chair by fireplace; settee, left, towards front; and a long oak stool in the window.

The various properties are described or implied in the text of the play.

THE FIRST ACT

THE SERVANT IN THE HOUSE

THE FIRST ACT

As the curtain ascends, Rogers and Manson are discovered laying the table for breakfast, the lad being at the upper end of the table, facing the audience, Manson, with his back to the audience, being at the lower end. Rogers is an ordinary little cockney boy in buttons; Manson is dressed in his native Eastern costume. His face is not seen until the point indicated lower down.

ROGERS [glancing across curiously]. Arskin' your pardon, Mr. Manson. . . .

MANSON. Yes: what is it, Rogers?

ROGERS. Funny thing—cawn't get it out of my 'ead as I've knowed you somewhere before. Don't scarcely seem possible, do it, Mr. Manson?

MANSON. Many things are possible in this world, Rogers.

ROGERS. That's all right; but 'ow long 'av' you been in England, Mr. Manson?

MANSON. I landed late last night, if that's what you mean.

ROGERS. Well, I never been in the continong of Asia, where you come from; and there you are!

MANSON [quietly]. Yes: here I am.

> [He goes to the sideboard and busies himself with serviettes, mats, etc.]

ROGERS. Perhaps it's this reincarnytion the Daily Mail been writing about. Ever see the Daily Mail out there, Mr. Manson?

MANSON. No: we had few advantages.

ROGERS. Rum idea, reincarnytion! Think, Mr. Manson, perhaps we wos lords once in ancient Babylon, you an' me!

MANSON. And now butler and page-boy, eh?

ROGERS [scratching his head]. Does seem a bit of a come-down, don't it?

MANSON. That's one way of looking at it.

> [ROGERS, enticed of Satan, has conveyed a furtive spoonful of jam towards his mouth.]

[Without turning.] Isn't there jam in the kitchen, Rogers?

ROGERS [scared]. Evings! E've got eyes in 'is boots! S'y, do you call it stealing, Mr. Manson?

MANSON. Do you? [Persisting.] Do you?

[ROGERS drops the spoon and moves
mournfully away from temptation.]

ROGERS. 'Pon my word, Mr. Manson, you give
me the fair creeps and no mistike!

MANSON. You will get over that when you know
me better.

ROGERS. Mr. Manson! Do you mind if I arst
you a question?

MANSON. No; what is it?

ROGERS. What d'you wear them togs for? This
ain't India.

MANSON. People don't always recognise me in
anything else.

[He turns for the first time. His face
is one of awful sweetness, dignity,
and strength. There is the calm of
a great mastery about him, suited
to his habit as a servant.]

ROGERS. Garn, Mr. Manson, that's a bit orf!
Clothes don't make all that difference, come now! . . .

MANSON. They are the only things the people of
this world see.

ROGERS [after a pause]. Excuse me, Mr. Manson,
you mek me larf.

MANSON. That's all right, Rogers. I have a
sense of humour myself, or I shouldn't be here.

ROGERS [suddenly sentimental]. Talking about clothes, Mr. Manson, I often thinks in my 'ead as I'd like to be a church clergyman, like master. Them strite-up collars are very becoming. Wouldn't you, Mr. Manson?

MANSON. Wouldn't that be rather presuming, Rogers?

ROGERS. Don't you mek no mistike about it! 'Ere! [He grows confidential.] *You are* a butler, ain't you? Ain't you, now? . . .

MANSON. Something like that.

ROGERS. Well, perhaps master 'asn't allus been as 'igh— See! O' course, I don't know, but they *do* s'y as 'e was once only a . . . Wot oh! 'Ere 'e is!

[The VICAR's voice is heard off.]

VICAR. I shall be in to breakfast at a quarter to nine. Don't wait for me, dearest.

> [He enters hurriedly from door, right, watch in hand. He has on his cassock and biretta.]

So awkward— Both my curates down with the whooping-cough! To-day, too! Just when I was expecting . . .

> [As he goes up stage, left of table, MANSON comes down, right, with serviettes. The VICAR wheels round

slowly, facing him. Observing his
astonishment, ROGERS steps forward
with explanation.]

ROGERS. It's the new butler, sir. Mr. Manson,
sir.

VICAR. Surely, I—I've seen you somewhere before.

MANSON [looking at him]. Have you, sir?

VICAR. Hm! No, I can't quite . . .

ROGERS. Beg pardon, sir: getting on for eight.

   [He hands him a small silver paten
   upon which there is a piece of
   bread.]

VICAR [Taking it mechanically]. Hm! These
mysteries are not always helpful . . . Anyway, I'm
glad to see you, Manson. When did you arrive?

   [He begins to break the bread into
   fragments whilst talking.]

MANSON. Early this morning, sir. I should have
come sooner; but I had a little trouble down at the
Customs.

VICAR. Indeed! How was that?

MANSON. They said something about the new
Alien Act, sir.

VICAR. Of course, of course. Er . . . You speak
English remarkably well.

[21]

MANSON. I have seen a good deal of the English, one time and another.

VICAR. That's good; it will save a lot of explanation. By-the-bye . . .

My old friend in Brindisi, who recommended you, writes that you bore a very excellent character with your late employer in India; but there was one matter he didn't mention— No doubt you will recognise its importance in a clergyman's family— He never mentioned your religion.

MANSON. I can soon remedy that, sir. My religion is very simple. I love God and all my brothers.

VICAR [after a pause]. God and your brothers . . .

MANSON. Yes, sir; *all* of them.

> [The VICAR stands thoughtful for a moment. He places the paten on the table, beside him.]

VICAR [slowly]. That is not always so easy, Manson; but it is my creed, too.

MANSON. Then— Brother!

> [Rapt in thought, the VICAR takes his proffered hand mechanically.]
> [MARY enters. She is a slim young girl in her teens, the picture of rosy sweetness and health.]

MARY. Good-morning, Uncle William! Oh! . . .

THE MOST REVEREND THE LORD BISHOP

I suppose you're Manson? I must say you look simply ripping! How do you do? My name's Mary. [She offers her hand.]

MANSON [kissing it]. A very dear name, too!

MARY [embarrassed, blurting]. We were wondering last night about your religion. I said . . .

VICAR. Mary, my child . . .

MARY. You don't *look* like a cannibal. After all, even the devil isn't as black as he's . . . Oh, I beg your pardon: perhaps I'm rude.

VICAR. Yes, indeed you are. Don't take any notice of our little feather-brain, Manson.

MARY. I say, has uncle told you who's coming to-day?

MANSON. No.

MARY. Not about Uncle Josh?

VICAR. T-t-t! You mustn't call your uncle Joshua that! It is irreverent. He may resent it.

MARY. You know, *you'll* make me positively dislike him! Just fancy, Manson, meeting an uncle whom you've never so much as set eyes on before! I don't even know what he looks like.

> [She is looking MANSON in the face. He returns her gaze curiously.]

MANSON. Then—you have a surprise in store.

MARY. *You* ought to be awfully interested! You will, when you hear where he comes from!

MANSON. I *am*—interested.

MARY. Then guess who he is!

MANSON. Guess—when I know already?

MARY. Oh, Uncle Joshua isn't his *only* name— don't you think that! He's a very important person, *I* can tell you! His name's on everybody's lips!

MANSON [dryly]. Really!

MARY. Can't you guess? . . . Think of the very biggest person you ever heard of in this world!

MANSON. In *this* world: that sounds rather like . . . Does he give free libraries?

MARY. I can't say I ever heard of that; but he does things quite as wonderful! Listen! What do you think of the BISHOP OF BENARES!!

MANSON [unimpressed]. Oh, it's the—Bishop of Benares, is it?

MARY. I must say, you don't seem very surprised! Surely you've heard of him? He *comes* from India.

MANSON [quietly]. I happen to know him.

VICAR. No, really: this is most interesting!

MANSON. As a man might know *his own soul*, sir— as they say in India. His work has been mine, so to speak.

VICAR. Bless me, you will know him better than I

do. I have never seen him since I was quite a little lad.

MARY [with prodigious solemnity]. Just you think, Manson! He's my uncle—my own father's brother!

> [MANSON is now up stage between the two.]

MANSON. *Your* brother, sir?

VICAR [fervently]. I am grateful to God for it, Manson: he is.

> [MANSON regards him calmly for a moment: then he turns inquiringly towards Mary.]

MANSON. Then—Miss Mary? . . .

VICAR [quickly]. Oh, my niece is the daughter of —of my other brother.

MANSON. I see: *two* brothers?

VICAR [shortly]. Yes, yes, I have: I—I had.

MANSON [resuming his work at the table]. Thank you, sir: it's always helpful, coming to a new place, to know who are—and who are not—the family connections.

VICAR. Come, Rogers! My poor brethren in the church are waiting. I must see to their necessities at once. [He starts for the door.]

MANSON. Pardon me, sir.

> [He hands him the bread which,

> among those necessities, he has for-
> gotten. The VICAR looks at him a
> moment in troubled thought, and
> then goes out, followed by ROGERS.]

ROGERS [at door]. I'll be back to 'elp you in with the breakfast, Mr. Manson.   [Exit.]

MARY. Now, Manson: let's talk! You've got nothing more to do? . . .

MANSON. Not till breakfast.

MARY. Then come over here, and make ourselves comfy.

> [They go over to the settee: she
> plumps herself down, gathering her
> legs up into a little bunch. He
> seats himself beside her.]

Now! Tell me everything you know about the Bishop of Benares!

MANSON. What—Uncle Josh?

MARY. Ssh — ssh — ssh! That's naughty, you know! You heard what Uncle William said! . . . Do you think he'd very much mind if I called him Uncle Josh?

MANSON. You may take it from *me*, that you may call him whatever you like.

MARY. That's all very well; but you're not Uncle Joshua!

MANSON. No? . . .

MARY [hotly]. No, you're not!

MANSON. Well, since you're so certain . . .

MARY [with conviction]. I'm perfectly certain he'll never stand a kid like me cheeking him and calling him names! Uncle William's quite right! . . . And that's why I've made up my mind that I sha'n't like him, after all!

MANSON. Indeed, I hope you will!

MARY. Do you believe in liking people simply because they're uncles?

MANSON. Perhaps I'm a prejudiced person.

MARY. I know exactly what he'll be—goody-goody, isn't he? You know — religious, and all that!

MANSON. God forbid!

MARY [fearfully]. Oh, perhaps he's the other sort—like auntie's brother! He's a bishop—the Bishop of Lancashire. You see, I've heard a lot about bishops in my time, and they're not always quite nice men.

MANSON. And what sort is the Bishop of Lancashire?

MARY. Well, I don't think I ought to tell you; but I once heard *Uncle William* call him a devil!—And he's a clergyman!

MANSON. Your Uncle Joshua's reputation is exactly opposite.

MARY. There is that: everybody speaks awfully well of him.

MANSON. I don't think I would go so far as that: some people blackguard him abominably.

MARY. No!—Who?

MANSON. His clergy, chiefly.

MARY. His clergy! They must be dreadfully wicked men!

MANSON. No—only blind: perhaps, also, a little deaf. But between the two they manage to make his work very difficult.

MARY. Why? What do they do?

MANSON. It's partly what they do *not* do.

MARY. Oh, I see—lazy.

MANSON. Not precisely—they work: they are not idle; but they serve other masters.

MARY. Such as whom?

MANSON. The Bishop of Lancashire.

MARY [after a pause]. I always thought he was such a great success out there. The papers have been full of it—of the millions of people who follow him about: they say they almost worship him in some places. What kind of people are they?

MANSON. Just common people.

MARY. And then, all that talk of the great churches he built out there! . . .

MANSON. Churches?

MARY. Yes; didn't he?

MANSON. He built one.

MARY. What's it like?

MANSON. Those who have seen it say there is nothing like it on earth.

MARY [eagerly]. Have you seen it?

MANSON. I was there when he built it.

MARY. From the very beginning?

MANSON [solemnly]. From the beginning.

> [MARY pauses before speaking: then she says, slowly.]

MARY. I hope I *shall* like him. Is he—is he anything like you?

> [MANSON regards her silently for a moment.]

MANSON. How is it that you know so little about him?

MARY. Well, you see, I only heard yesterday.

MANSON. I thought you said his *name* was on everybody's *lips*.

MARY. You don't understand. I mean, I never knew that he had anything to do with *me*—that he was my father's brother.

MANSON. Didn't *he* know?

MARY. Who—father? Oh, you see, I . . . *I don't know my father* . . . . . .

Uncle William didn't know anything about it until yesterday.

MANSON. Hm! That is strange, too!

MARY. There's a bit of a mystery about it altogether. Would you like to hear? It is rather like a fairy-tale.

MANSON. It must be. Yes, do go on.

MARY. It was all through Uncle William's Restoration Fund. You see, our old church is in a perfectly rotten state of decay, and naturally it would take a lot to repair it: so uncle thought of starting a Fund—Yes! Wasn't it clever of him?—I addressed all the envelopes.

Would you believe it, we couldn't get a single halfpenny! Isn't it a shame?—Such a nice old church, too!

MANSON. How was that?

MARY. That's the question! People have been most rude! Oh, the letters we have had! The funny thing is, for all their fault-finding, they none of them agree with each other!—Some say the foundations are all wrong: some don't like the stained-glass windows; but if you ask me . . .

MANSON. Yes, what do you think?

MARY. Well, uncle won't hear of it; but I can't help thinking old Bletchley is right . . .

MANSON. Who's he?

MARY. Oh, he's a dreadfully wicked man, I know that— He's the quack doctor in the village: he's— he's *an atheist!* . . .

MANSON. Well, what does he think is the matter?

MARY. He says it's the DRAIN!

MANSON. The—the drain? . . .

MARY. Um! You know, in spite of what uncle says, there *is* a smell: I had it in my nose all last Sunday morning. Up in the choir it's bad enough, and round by the pulpit— Ugh! I can't think how uncle stands it!

That's why the people won't come to church— They *say* so: they stand in the market-place listening to old Bletchley, instead of listening to uncle and trying to be good.

The odd thing is, it must be that very same drain that's causing the trouble in uncle's study— That's his study out there, where they've been digging: it's where he writes his sermons. You know, *I've* noticed the smell for some time, but uncle got so cross whenever I mentioned it, that I learned to hold my tongue. At last, auntie smelt it, too, and that soon brought the men in! Ugh! Perhaps you've . . .

MANSON. I have!   But what has all this to do with . . .

MARY. Don't get impatient: it's all part of the story. . . . Well, we thought we should have poor dear Uncle William perfectly ill . . .

MANSON. Because of the drain? . . .

MARY. No, because of the Fund.   He tried everything: all his rich friends, bazaars, jumble-sales, special intercessions—everything!   And nothing seemed to come of it!

Then at last, yesterday morning, he was reading the newspaper, and there was a long piece about the Bishop of Benares. Uncle read it aloud to us. Suddenly, in the middle, he broke off and said: *Look at the power this chap seems to have at the back of him!   I wish to God I had some of it!*

He had scarcely said it, when there was a rat-tat at the door: it was the postman; and what do you think? IT WAS A LETTER FROM THE BISHOP OF BENARES!

MANSON [anticipating the critics]. What a coincidence!

MARY. Isn't that wonderful?   *Isn't* it just like a fairy-tale?   Wait a bit.   There's more yet . . .

[32]

Here's the letter: uncle gave it me for my autographs . . .

> [She fishes it out from her pocket.
> MANSON reads it aloud, slowly and
> clearly.]

MANSON. *"I shall be with you during to-morrow morning. If any one will help me, I will restore your church. Your brother, Joshua."*

MARY [pointing]. And there, do you see, underneath, in brackets: *The Bishop of Benares.*

MANSON. Dear me, dear me, just those few words!

MARY. Wasn't it like an answer to prayer? Auntie saw that at once!

And the odd part about it is, that Uncle William *did* have a brother Joshua who went away and got lost in India years and years ago! And to think that he was *who* he was all the time! To think of him never writing until yesterday! To think that before the day is out he will be sitting down here, perhaps in this very place, just like . . .

> [She breaks off suddenly, gazing at
> him; for his eyes have taken a
> strange fire.]

MANSON. Just like I am now . . .

MARY [falteringly]. Yes . . .

MANSON. Talking to you . . .

[33]

MARY. Oh! . . . [She rises, afraid.]

MANSON [softly]. Mary . . .

MARY [in a whisper]. Who are you? . . .

MANSON. I am . . .

> [He is interrupted by the great bell
> of the church, which tolls the Sanctus.
> After the third stroke, he continues.]

I am the servant in this house. I have my work
to do. Would you like to help me?

MARY. What shall I do?

MANSON. Help to spin the fairy-tale. Will you?

MARY. I will.

MANSON. Then keep the secret — Remember!
And wish hard.

MARY. Do you believe in wishing?

MANSON. Everything comes true, if you wish
hard enough.

MARY. What shall I wish for?

MANSON. What have you needed most? What
have you not had? Think it out.

> [Enter AUNTIE in a négligée morning
> gown. She has a preoccupied air.
> She carries her husband's coat over
> her arm.]

AUNTIE. Oh, I heard you had arrived. I hope
they gave you something to eat when you came in.

[34]

MANSON. Thank you, ma'am: it will do later.

AUNTIE. Mary . . . Dearest . . .

MARY. Oh, I beg your pardon, auntie dear, I . . .

AUNTIE. Dreaming again! [Putting her arm round her.] Come, I want you to put your uncle's coat by the fire. He will be cold, coming out of that draughty church.

MARY [hugging her]. You darling! I believe you think of nobody but uncle in the world!

AUNTIE. And you, sweetheart: you come next— a very near next! Now, run along.

[MARY takes the coat to the fire.]

[Surveying the table]. That's very nice, Manson, very nice indeed! Perhaps, just a little further this way. . . . [Removes flowers.] My husband is so fond of them. Ye-es; and I *wanted* things *particularly* nice this morning . . .

MARY [at the fire, looking up]. I thought you said you—you didn't expect him till twelve-thirty! . . .

AUNTIE [absorbed]. Whom?

MARY [chuckling]. The—the Bishop of Benares.

AUNTIE. The — the . . . Oh, it's your *uncle* I am . . . [To Manson]. By-the-bye, has the postman been yet?

MANSON [at the window]. I can see him coming up the lane. He's stopped at the next house.

AUNTIE. Oh, then, Mary: will you very much mind if you don't have breakfast with us this morning? I want to have a private talk with your uncle.

MARY. Oh, auntie, dear! . . .

AUNTIE. Don't think of yourself, dear— Remember, there are other people in the world besides you. Go down into the village, and have breakfast with poor old Grannie Durden. Take her some nice new-laid eggs and a pat of butter— Poor soul, it would be a charity!

MARY. Oh, auntie, she's as deaf as a post!

AUNTIE. Dearest!— Remember what your uncle said last Sunday about *Pure religion and undefiled!* He mentioned Mrs. Durden only a week ago; but I forgot. Now, run along.

MARY [reluctantly]. Very well, auntie.

[She goes out by the main door.]

AUNTIE [laughing]. Inconsiderate little monkey! I am glad you have not thought of changing your pretty, native costume, Manson. It is very picturesque; and, besides, to-day there is a special reason why it may be considered complimentary.

[A double knock is heard at the outer door.]

Ah! Quick, Manson! The postman!

[MANSON goes out. AUNTIE takes

[36]

> a look at the coat: rearranges the
> flowers, humming, meanwhile, "The
> Church's One Foundation"; and
> then stands impatiently awaiting
> MANSON's reappearance. Presently
> he returns with a letter on server.]

MANSON. A letter for you, ma'am.

AUNTIE. Ah! What I expected!

> [She breaks open the letter and reads
> it eagerly.]

Excellent! [More dubiously]. Excellent . . .

Manson, we shall have to be very busy to-day.
There will be quite a Church Congress to lunch—two
bishops!

MANSON. Oh, not as bad as that, ma'am!

AUNTIE. Manson!

MANSON. Beg pardon, ma'am; but master mentioned only one—his brother, the Bishop of Benares.

AUNTIE. *My* brother will join us also—the Bishop
of Lancashire. This is his letter.

And now let's have breakfast, at once. The vicar
is sure to be earlier than he said; and I'm hungry.

> [MANSON goes to the door. As he
> opens it, the VICAR and ROGERS re-
> appear.]

[37]

MANSON. Here is master.   I'll hurry up the breakfast, ma'am.

VICAR [entering]. Do, Manson.   Let's get it over.
[MANSON goes out.]

Excuse me, my dear.
[ROGERS helps him off with the
cassock.]

So tiresome!   Not a place in the house to do anything!   Confound the drains!   Just run up-stairs
for my coat, Rogers.

AUNTIE. It's here, dear.   I have it warming for
you.

VICAR [more graciously]. Oh, thank you, Martha.
That will do, then, Rogers.   Tell Manson to hurry up.
[ROGERS helps him on and goes out.
The cassock is left lying on the long
stool by the window.]
[The VICAR crosses moodily to the
fireplace.   AUNTIE stands undecid-
ed, watching him, the letter in her
hand.]

AUNTIE. You're back early, dear.

VICAR. What can you expect?   Not a soul there,
of course!

AUNTIE. My poor William!   I'm glad I thought
to hurry up the breakfast.

[38]

THE VICAR

VICAR. Thanks, dear. You are always thoughtful.

AUNTIE. William . . .

[He looks up.]

I—I want to have a little talk with you.

VICAR. What is it? Any more—worry?

AUNTIE. You needn't make it so.

VICAR. Ah!

AUNTIE [moving over to him and stroking his hair]. My dearest is not well.

VICAR. I think you are right, Martha. I am *not* well.

AUNTIE [alarmed]. Not the trouble with your heart again?

VICAR. No; I fancy it goes deeper than that!

AUNTIE. William! What do you mean?

VICAR [suddenly facing her]. Martha! Do you know the sort of man you have been living with all these years? Do you see through me? Do you know me?—No: don't speak: I see your answer already—Your own love blinds you! Ha! I am a *good man!*—I don't drink, I don't swear, I am respectable, I don't blaspheme like Bletchley! Oh yes, and I am a *scholar:* I can cackle in Greek: I can wrangle about God's name: I know Latin and Hebrew and all the cursed little pedantries of my

trade! But do you know what I am? Do you
know what your husband is in the sight of God?
He is a LIAR!

AUNTIE. William!

VICAR. A liar! I heard it in my ears as I stood
up before Christ's altar in the church this morning,
reciting my miserable creed! I heard it in my pray-
ers! I heard it whilst I tasted . . . whilst I drank . . .
whilst I . . .

> [He sinks into a chair, and buries his
> face in his hands.]

AUNTIE. Oh, you are ill!

VICAR [breaking down]. O wretched man that I
am! Who shall deliver me out of the body of this
death?

> [She stands above him, hesitating.
> After a moment, she says, deter-
> minedly.]

AUNTIE. I know: it's this money trouble. It's
what Joshua said in his letter about your having to
get somebody to help him. Well, that's just what
I wanted to speak to you about. I have a way out
of the difficulty.

VICAR. It's not the church. I could wish every
stone of it were crumbled into dust!

AUNTIE. William, how wicked of you! . . .

Is it — is it anything to do with your brother Joshua? Why don't you answer?

VICAR. *It has to do with my brother—Robert.*

AUNTIE. Mary's fa . . .

William, did you send him that telegram yesterday?

VICAR. Yes: that was a lie, too!

AUNTIE. Nonsense! Don't be absurd!

VICAR. It was a lie!

AUNTIE. You told him we couldn't do with him because the house was upset: that's true! You told him that the drains were up in the study: that's true!

VICAR. Was that the real reason why we refused to have him here? Was it?

AUNTIE. I can't think what possessed him to write and say he'd come. We've not heard from him for fifteen years!

VICAR. Whose fault is that?

AUNTIE. Why, his own, of course! He can't expect to be treated decently! [She walks up and down with anger.] It's perfectly absurd, it really is, dear, making all this fuss and trouble about a wretched—

Have you told Mary?

VICAR. No: the *silent* lie was comparatively easy!

AUNTIE. My dear, do try and be reasonable. Think of what he is!

VICAR. Isn't he my brother?

AUNTIE. No, he's not your brother—at least, nothing that a brother ought to be! Ridicules everything that you hold sacred! Hates everything you love! Loves everything you hate! . . .

VICAR. *That's* true!

AUNTIE. A scoffer, an atheist, a miserable drunkard!

VICAR. That was fifteen years ago, remember, after Mary's mother died! . . .

AUNTIE. A man like that never changes! What would have become of that poor child if we hadn't stepped in? Have you ever dared to tell her what her father's like? Of course not! To-day, too, of all days! It's utterly preposterous!

VICAR. That is all the more reason why . . .

AUNTIE. My dear, think of his *occupation!*

VICAR. I think the child ought to be told.

AUNTIE. Of his *occupation?*

VICAR. That, and everything.

AUNTIE. My dear, have you gone perfectly mad? Do you know who's coming? Do you want to advertise his *occupation* to all the world?

VICAR. Do you think his brother Joshua would mind that?

AUNTIE. It isn't only your brother Joshua! You think of nobody but your brother Joshua! Some one else is coming.

VICAR. Who?

AUNTIE. *My brother James!* [She throws down the letter.] Now you've heard it all!

[There is a long silence. Then the
VICAR speaks in a low, intense voice
of bitter contempt.]

VICAR. Your brother James is coming here to-day? You have brought him here to help my brother Joshua! *Him!*

AUNTIE. Why not? He's rich! He can do it!

VICAR. So, he can recognise me at last!

AUNTIE. It was as much your fault as his, that you have never met! He naturally resented our marriage.

VICAR [ironically]. But, of course, now that I'm related to the great and *wealthy* Bishop of Benares . . .

AUNTIE [warmly]. He's as much a bishop as your brother is!

VICAR. He! That gaitered snob!

AUNTIE. William, how dare you!

VICAR. Yes, he's a bishop! A bishop of stocks and shares! A bishop of the counting-house! A bishop of Mammon!

AUNTIE. William!

VICAR. The devil's own bishop!

AUNTIE. *At least, he isn't a* WORKING-MAN!

VICAR [as though stung]. Ah! . . .

> [They stand below the table, one on either side, tense with passion. They remain so.]
>
> [MANSON and ROGERS come in with the breakfast. ROGERS goes out immediately.]

MANSON. Sorry to have delayed, sir; but you said a quarter to nine, didn't you, sir?

VICAR. Yes.

MANSON. Breakfast's served, ma'am.   It's served, sir.

> [They move to the table, absently, first one, then the other, as he goes to each separately.]
>
> [MANSON serves them in silence for a few moments.]

Beg pardon, sir: what time did you expect the Bishop of Benares?

VICAR. Oh!—*During the morning*, he said.   That will mean the twelve-thirty, I suppose.   It's the only convenient service.

MANSON. And the Bishop of Lancashire, ma'am?

AUNTIE. He didn't say; but I think we may expect him by the same train. He would scarcely think of catching the . . .

[There is heard a loud Ringing of the Bell—a bishop at the very least. All three heads turn automatically.]

Good gracious! Already!

MANSON. It doesn't sound like the Bishop of Benares, ma'am. He generally comes very quietly.

AUNTIE. Quick!

MANSON. Yes, ma'am.

[He goes out by the main door.]

AUNTIE [rapidly]. William, I'm sorry! Really, I didn't mean you: I never thought of you: I was only thinking of Robert. I only think of you as a great scholar and a saint—yes, you are one!—and as the man I love! I would sacrifice everything to your happiness. Robert's nothing to me: that's why I . . . Think of what it might mean to Mary—we must think of others, William!—our own little child, as we try to imagine . . .

[The VICAR makes a gesture of anguish.]

As for James, God knows I did it for the best. I love you, my dear, I love you: I wouldn't have vexed you for the world! After all, he *is* my brother,

William! . . . . I thought of patching up the enmity between you: I thought of all your hopes of rebuilding the church; and James was the only rich man I thought might be induced—under the circumstances . . .

VICAR. I am in the darkness. I don't know what to do. God has left me stranded.

> [MANSON re-enters. They look at him inquiringly.]

MANSON. It isn't the Bishop of Benares, ma'am.

AUNTIE. Well, who is it?

MANSON. I didn't ask his name, ma'am.

AUNTIE. T-t-t! How is he dressed?

MANSON. Rather oddly, ma'am: I noticed that his legs . . .

AUNTIE. William, it's James! I can't be seen like this. Shew him in. I can slip out this way.

> [MANSON goes out.]

William, try and treat him like . . .

VICAR. How? Like a brother?

AUNTIE. I was going to say, like a Priest and a Christian, William.

VICAR. Like a Christian, then.

AUNTIE. My dear!

> [She goes out by the door to the right, as MANSON begins to turn the handle of the other door.]

[46]

MANSON [outside]. This way, if you please.

> [The VICAR braces himself up and turns towards the door with an effort at cordiality.]

VICAR. Just in time for breakfast, my lord.

> [Enter ROBERT SMITH and MANSON. ROBERT'S costume is a navvy's, the knees tied with string.]

ROBERT [grimly]. Thanks, Bill Awlmighty, don't mind if I do.   My belly's fair aching.

VICAR. Robert!

ROBERT. Yus, it's me, my 'oly brother!

VICAR. Didn't you—didn't you get my wire?

ROBERT. Yus, I gorit: *Drains wrong*, eh ? Thought I'd like to 'av' a look at 'em—my job, yer know, *drains!*   So you'll excuse the togs: remind you of old days, eh what ?

VICAR. Robert, what have you come here for?

ROBERT. *You* arsk me that ?

VICAR. Yes, I do, Bob . . .

ROBERT. Why, to see my little gel, o' course— Gawd curse you! . . .

Now go an tell your ole woman.

> [The VICAR stands as though stricken.]

Did you 'ear me speak ?   Tell 'er!

[The VICAR wavers a moment, and
then staggers out silently through
the door, right. ROBERT watches
him off with a look of iron. He pays
no heed to MANSON, who stands
quite close to him, on the left.]

See that blighter? That's the bloke as was born
with no bowels! 'E might a-made a man o' me once,
if 'e'd tried; but 'e didn't—'im and 'is like. Hm!
Dam foolish, I call it, don't you?

MANSON. Yes, both: foolish and—damned!

[ROBERT turns and looks into his
face for the first time as the curtain
slowly falls on the First Act.]

THE SECOND ACT

THE SECOND ACT

As the curtain rises, the scene and situation remain unchanged. Presently, Robert, having completed his inspection of the other's face and costume, moves away with a characteristic interjection.

ROBERT. Oh, Jeeroosalem! . . .
'Ere, 'elp us orf, comride: I'm wet through. Rainin' cats an' dorgs dahn at the Junction! 'Ere, I cawn't . . . Wot oh! The very identical! . . .

> [MANSON has helped him off with his coat, and now hands him the cassock.]

[Getting into it.] Don't know oo you are, ole pal; but you're a bit of orl right! . . . Don't I look a corf-drop? 'Ere, where ye teking it to? . . .

> [He watches MANSON suspiciously as he places his coat before the fire to dry.]

Bit 'andy, ain't yer? . . .
So this is where 'e lives! A bloomin' palace, as never I *did* see! . . .

[51]

[MANSON prepares a place for him
at the table, and pours out a cup of
tea, etc.]

Right you are, ole comride! 'E said breakfast, an'
breakfast it shall be, I don't fink! Blimey! Sossingers! Ain't 'ad the taste of sossingers in my gizzard
for I don't know 'ow long!

[He sits and devours whilst MANSON
breaks and hands him bread, waiting upon him.]

[Between bites.] Wouldn't think as I was 'is
brother, would yer — not to look at me? But
strooth, *I am;* an' wot's more, 'e cawn't deny it! . . .
[He labours with a little joke.] There's a lot o' brothers
knockin' abaht as people don't know on, eh what?
See wot I mean? [Suddenly serious.] Not as I'm
one o' them sort, mind yer: my father married my
mother honest, same as I married my little . . .

[After a moment's reflection, he
makes fresh onslaught upon the
sausages. Presently he looks up.]

'Ere, ain't you goin' ter 'av' none? . . .
Cawn't yer speak?

MANSON. Yes.

ROBERT. Well, why cawn't yer arnser a bloke
when 'e arsks yer civil?

[52]

MANSON. You didn't make it clear that you wanted to eat with me.

ROBERT. Want a bit of 'eart in it, eh?

MANSON. Yes, that's all.

ROBERT [largely]. Sit dahn, ole pal! Mek yourself at 'ome!

[MANSON obeys.]

See, wot was I tawkin' abaht, just afore you turned narsty?

MANSON. You were going to say something about —your little girl's mother.

[ROBERT'S cutlery bristles up like bayonets.]

ROBERT. Look 'ere, mate, don't you come tryin' it on with me! I don't care *oo* you are!

MANSON. I know that.

ROBERT. Then let me be, I tell yer! You tek all the taste out o' my sossingers.

MANSON. I should like to hear about her, comrade.

ROBERT. *You* cawn't bring 'er back. She's dead.

MANSON. What was her name?

ROBERT. Mary—same as the little gel's.

MANSON. I wonder whether they are anything alike.

ROBERT. That's wot I come to see! . . .

She 'ad 'er mother's nose when she was a biby—
and 'er eyes! Gorstrike, she was the very spit—far
as a biby could be! . . .

Swelp me Moses, if I find 'er anything like Bill's
ole geezer, I'll cut 'er throat!

MANSON. And if she's like her mother? What then?

ROBERT. Why, then . . . there's allus my own. I
nearly did it once.

MANSON [after a pause]. How did you come to
lose her?

ROBERT [roughly]. Never you mind!

MANSON. How did you come to lose her?

ROBERT [sullenly]. Typhoid fever.

> [MANSON notes the evasion with a
> glance. He helps ROBERT to more
> tea, and waits for him to speak.
> ROBERT wriggles under his gaze,
> and at last he says, reluctantly.]

Oh, it was my own fault, as I lost *the kid!*

MANSON. That was a sore loss, comrade.

ROBERT. *I* know it! Needn't rub it in! . . .

Look 'ere, comride, I 'adn't a bad nature to begin with. Didn't me an' my brother Joshua pinch
an' slave the skin orf our bones to send that spotted
swine to school? Didn't we 'elp 'im out with 'is
books an' 'is mortar-boards an' 'is bits of clothes to

try an' mek 'im look respectable? That's wot *we* did, till 'e got 'is lousy scholyships, an' run away to get spliced with that she-male pup of a blood-'ound! Cos why? Cos we was proud of the little perisher!— proud of 'is 'ead-piece! We 'adn't gone none ourselves—leastways, *I* 'adn't: Joshua was different to me; and now . . .

MANSON. And your brother Joshua: what of him? Where is *he* now?

ROBERT. *I* don't know — gone to pot, like me! P'r'aps eatin' is bleedin' 'eart out, same as I am, at the base ingratitood of the world!

MANSON. Perhaps so!

ROBERT. Where was I? You mek me lose my air, shoving in with your bit!

MANSON. You were saying that you hadn't a bad nature to begin with.

ROBERT [truculently]. No more I 'adn't! . . .

O' course, when she took an'—an' died, things was different: I couldn't 'old up the same— Some-'ow, I don't know, I lost my 'eart, and . . .

MANSON. Yes? . . .

ROBERT. That's 'ow I come to lose my kid, my little kid . . . Mind you, that was fifteen years ago: I was a rotter then, same as you might be. I wasn't 'arf the man I am now . . .

You can larf! A man can change a lot in fifteen years!

MANSON. *I* didn't laugh.

ROBERT. Do you want to know wot's come over me since then? I *work*—and work well: that's more than some of 'em can say— And I don't get much money for it, either! That ought to mek 'em feel ashamed! I'm not the drunkard I was—not by 'arf! If I'm bitter, oo's made me bitter? You cawn't be very sweet and perlite on eighteen bob a week—*when yer get it!* I'll tell yer summat else: I've eddicated myself since then—I'm not the gory fool I was— *And* they know it! They can't come playin' the 'anky with us, same as they used to! It's *Nice Mister Working-man This and Nice Mister Working-man That, will yer be so 'ighly hobliging as to 'and over your dear little voting-paper*—you poor, sweet, muddy-nosed old idiot, as can't spot your natural enemy when yer see 'im! That orter mek some on 'em sit up!

Fifteen years ago me an' my like 'adn't got a religion! By Gawd, we 'av' one now! Like to 'ear wot it is?

MANSON. Yes.

ROBERT. SOCIALISM! Funny, ain't it?

MANSON. *I* don't think so. It's mine, too.

AUNTIE

ROBERT. I believe in fighting with my clarss!

MANSON. Oh, against whom?

ROBERT. Why, agin all the other clarsses—curse 'em!

MANSON. Isn't that a bit of the old Robert left, comrade?

ROBERT. Oh, leave me alone. I cawn't be allus pickin' an' choosin' my words! I ain't no scholar—thank Gawd!

MANSON. All the same, I'm right, eh, comrade? Comrade . . .

ROBERT [grudgingly]. Well, yus! [Savagely.] Yus, I tell yer! Cawn't a bloke speak 'otter than 'e means without *you* scrapin' at 'is innards?

[Exploding again). Wait till I set eyes on that bleedin' brother of mine again, that's all!

MANSON. Which bleeding brother?

ROBERT [with a thumb-jerk). Why, *'im*, o' course! [Sneering.] The Reverend William! 'Im as you said was damned! . . . Allus did 'ate parsons! I 'ates the sight of their 'arf-baked, silly mugs!

> [There is a very loud Ringing of the Bell.]

'Ello! 'Ello! Did I mek a row like that?

MANSON. You tried, didn't you?

ROBERT. So I did, not 'arf! Thought if I kicked

up an 'ell of a shindy they'd think some big bug was comin'; and then when they'd be all smiles an' bowin' an' scrapin', in pops me, real low!

> [ROGERS enters. On seeing them at the table, he is apparently troubled with his inside.]

ROGERS. Oh, my 'oly Evings!

MANSON. Who is it, Rogers?

ROGERS [awed]. It's the Bishop of Lancashire!

MANSON [imperturbably]. Shew him in, Rogers.

ROGERS. Beg pardon, Mr. Manson . . .

MANSON. I said, shew him in.

Quick, Rogers. Keep a bishop waiting!

ROGERS. Well, I'm jiggered!

> [He is; and goes out.]

ROBERT. 'Ere! Did 'e say *bishop?*

MANSON. Yes.

ROBERT. Comin' 'ere? Now?

> [MANSON nods his head to each inquiry.]

Well, I ain't agoin' ter leave my sossingers, not if 'e was a bloomin' archangel, see!

> [ROGERS, still jiggered, ushers in JAMES PONSONBY MAKESHYFTE, D.D., the Most Reverend the Lord Bishop of Lancashire. He looks his

name, his goggles and ear-trumpet lending a beautiful perfection to the resemblance.]

[Manson has risen: Robert, imperturbable, discusses sossingers: Rogers, with a last excruciation of his ailment, vanishes.]

[The Most Reverend Father in God stands blinking for recognition. Pained at the non-fulfilment of this worthy expectation, he moves—a little blindly—towards the table. Here he encounters the oppugnant back of the voracious Robert, who grows quite annoyed. Indeed, he as good as says so.]

'Ere, where ye comin' to?

Bishop [peering closely into his face, the other edging away]. Ah! Mr. Smythe, or I am mistaken.

Robert. Smith's my name! Don't you call me Smythe!

Bishop. My dear sir, don't mention it: my sister has explained everything. I bear you no grudge—none whatever!

Robert. What's the silly ole josser jawin' abaht now?

[59]

BISHOP. But I perceive that I have—er—[sniffing] disturbed you at your morning meal . . .

ROBERT [with conviction]. You 'av' that!

BISHOP. Eh? . . .

ROBERT [louder]. I say, you 'av'!

BISHOP [fixing his ear-trumpet]. Just once more . . .

ROBERT. Oh, Moses! [Roaring, and indicating his breakfast.] You 'av', blarst you!

BISHOP [mistaking the gesticulation]. Thank you, you are very kind. I think I will. I could get nothing on the journey but a cup of coffee and a bun.

> [He sits at the table without ever having perceived MANSON, who has nevertheless been serving him.]

ROBERT. Yus, you look as if you fed on buns!

> [Throughout the play the audience will understand where the BISHOP does, and where he does not, hear by his use or non-use of the ear-trumpet. Perhaps the reader will be good enough to imagine these occasions for himself, as he may have observed a reluctance on the part of the author to encumber the text with stage directions.]

[60]

BISHOP [eating, and at the same time addressing the becassocked ROBERT]. And you must not think, on account of the little coolness between us, that I have not followed your career with great interest— very great interest! Your scholastic achievements have been most praiseworthy—especially under the unfortunate circumstances. . . . Although, by-the-way, I cannot at all agree with your gloss on Romans fourteen, twenty-three: *Katakekritai* either means *damned* or nothing at all.

ROBERT [gesticulating]. It was *'im* as said *damned!*

BISHOP. No, no, sir: it is perfectly indefensible!

ROBERT. I'll use what langwidge I like!

BISHOP [warming]. You said *katakekritai* . . .

ROBERT. I never did, *I* tek my oath!

BISHOP. My dear sir, I learned my Greek at Shrewsbury, before you were born! Don't argue, sir!

ROBERT. Oo is argufying? . . . Talking to me about yer Katama-what-d'you-call-it!

BISHOP. We had better drop the subject! . . . Bœotian! After all, it is not precisely the matter which has brought us together. And that reminds me . . . [Trumpet]. Has he come yet?

ROBERT. Oo?

BISHOP. Your brother, of course.

ROBERT. My brother! Oh, you'll see '*im* soon enough!

BISHOP. I gather from your remark that he has not arrived yet. Good! The fact is, I should like a preliminary discussion with yourself before meeting your illustrious brother.

ROBERT. Then you'd better look slippy!

BISHOP. I beg your pardon? . . .

ROBERT [with a flap at the trumpet]. Go on: you 'eard.

BISHOP. Of course, the *financial* undertaking is considerable: it's not like an *investment*, where there is some reasonable hope of a return: it's merely a matter of charity! The money's—gone, so to speak.

ROBERT. Yus, I've noticed that about money, myself.

BISHOP. At the same time, I should like my *name* to be associated with your brother's, in so worthy an enterprise . . .

ROBERT [mildly sarcastic]. You don't say!

BISHOP. And then again, I *trust*—I say I *trust*—I am not impervious to the more sacred obligations involved; but . . .

[He gropes blindly for bread.]

ROBERT. I allus notice that sort of 'igh talk ends with a "but" . . .

BISHOP. Naturally, I should like to learn a little, beforehand, of your brother's *views*. From what I gather, they are not altogether likely to coincide with my own. Of course, he is an idealist, a dreamer. Now, under these circumstances, perhaps . . .

Eh, what— Oh! Bless my soul!

> [MANSON has been offering him bread
> for some time. He has just tumbled
> to the fact of his presence. He rises.]

My—my Brother from Benares, I presume?

ROBERT. What, *my* pal, *'is* brother! Oh, Je'os-haphat!

BISHOP. Ten thousand pardons! Really, my eyesight is deplorable! Delighted to meet you! . . .

I was just observing to our charming host that— er— Humph! . . .

Bless me! Now what *was* I . . .

MANSON. Something about your sacred obligations, I believe.

BISHOP. May I trouble you again?

> [MANSON gravely fixes the ear-trum-
> pet in his ear.]

ROBERT. That's right: stick the damned thing in 'is ear-'ole, comride!

MANSON [through the trumpet]. Your sacred obligations.

[63]

BISHOP. Precisely, precisely! Er— Shall we sit?
[They do so. The BISHOP looks to
MANSON to begin. MANSON, failing
him, the spirit begins to work within
himself.]
Well—er—speaking of that, of course, my dearly-
beloved brother, I feel very seriously on the matter,
very seriously—as I am sure you do. The restoration of a church is a tremendous, an overwhelming
responsibility. To begin with, it—it costs quite a
lot. Doesn't it?

MANSON. It does: quite a lot.

BISHOP. Hm, yes—yes! . . . You mentioned *Sacred
obligations* just now, and I think that on the whole
I am inclined to agree with you. It is an admirable
way of putting it. We must awaken people to a
sense of their *sacred obligations*. This is a work in
which everybody can do something: the rich man
can give of the abundance with which it has pleased
Providence specially to favour him: the poor man
with his slender savings need have no fear for the
poverty of his gift— Let him give all: it will be
accepted. Those of us who, like yourself, my dear
brother—and I say it in all modesty, perhaps *my*self
—are in possession of the endowments of learning,
of influence, of authority—we can lend our *names* to

the good work. As you say so very beautifully: *sacred obligations.*

By-the-way, I don't think I quite caught your views as to the probable cost. Eh, what do you think?

MANSON. I think that should depend upon the obligations; and then, of course, the sacredness might count for something.

BISHOP. Yes, yes, we've discussed all that. But bringing it down to a *practical* basis: how much could we manage with?

MANSON. What do you say to—everything you have?

BISHOP. My dear sir, I'm not talking about myself!

MANSON. Well—everything the others have?

BISHOP. My dear sir, they're not fools! Do discuss the matter like a man of the world!

MANSON. *God's not watching: let's give as little, and grab as much as we can!*

BISHOP. Ssh! My dear brother! Remember who's present! [He glances toward Robert.] However . . . [Coughs.] We will return to this later. I begin to understand you.

ROBERT. Yus: you *think* you do!

BISHOP. At the same time, I do think we ought

to come to some general understanding: we must count the cost. Now, from all accounts, *you* have had some experience of church-building out in India —not that I think the extravagance for which you are credited would be either possible or desirable in this country—oh, no! Thank God, we know how to worship in spirit and in truth, without the aid of expensive buildings! However, I should like to hear your views. How did you manage it?

MANSON. Sacrifice.

BISHOP. Of course, of course; but *practically*. They say it's an enormous concern!

MANSON. So it is.

BISHOP. Well, what would such an establishment as that represent? In round numbers, now?

MANSON [calmly]. Numberless millions.

BISHOP. Numberless mil . . . ! [He drops his fork.] My dear sir, absurd! . . . Why, the place must be a palace—fit for a king!

MANSON. It is!

BISHOP. Do you mean to tell me that one man alone, on his own naked credit, could obtain numberless millions for such an object as that? How could you possibly get them together?

MANSON. They came freely from every quarter of the world.

BISHOP. On the security of your own name alone?

MANSON. No other, I assure you.

BISHOP. For Heaven's sake, tell me all about it! What sort of a place is it?

MANSON [seriously]. Are you quite sure you can hear?

BISHOP. Perhaps your voice is *not* quite so clear as it was. However . . .

> [He wipes the inside of the ear-trumpet, and fixes it afresh.]

Now! Tell me about your church.

> [During the following speech the BISHOP is occupied with his own thoughts: after the first few words he makes no attempt at listening: indeed, the trumpet goes down to the table again in no time. On the other hand, ROBERT, at first apathetic, gradually awakens to the keenest interest in what MANSON says.]

MANSON [very simply]. I am afraid you may not consider it an altogether substantial concern. It has to be seen in a certain way, under certain conditions. Some people never *see* it at all. You must understand, this is no dead pile of stones and unmeaning timber. *It is a living thing.*

BISHOP [in a hoarse whisper, self-engrossed]. Numberless millions!

MANSON. When you enter it you hear a sound—a sound as of some mighty poem chanted. Listen long enough, and you will learn that it is made up of the beating of human hearts, of the nameless music of men's souls—that is, if you have ears. If you have eyes, you will presently see the church itself—a looming mystery of many shapes and shadows, leaping sheer from floor to dome. The work of no ordinary builder!

BISHOP [trumpet down]. On the security of one man's name!

MANSON. The pillars of it go up like the brawny trunks of heroes: the sweet human flesh of men and women is moulded about its bulwarks, strong, impregnable: the faces of little children laugh out from every corner-stone: the terrible spans and arches of it are the joined hands of comrades; and up in the heights and spaces there are inscribed the numberless musings of all the dreamers of the world. It is yet building—building and built upon. Sometimes the work goes forward in deep darkness: sometimes in blinding light: now beneath the burden of unutterable anguish: now to the tune of a great laughter and heroic shoutings like the cry of thunder. [Softer.] Sometimes, in the silence of the night-time, one may hear the tiny hammerings of the comrades at work up in the dome—the comrades that have climbed ahead.

> [There is a short silence, broken only by the champing jaws of the BISHOP, who has resumed his sausages. ROBERT speaks first.]

ROBERT [slowly]. I think I begin to understand you, comride: especially that bit abaht . . . [his eyes stray upwards] . . . the 'ammerins' an' the—the harches—an' . . . Humph! I'm only an 'og! . . .

S'pose there's no drain 'ands wanted in that there church o' yours?

MANSON. Drains are a very important question there at present.

ROBERT. Why, I'd be cussin' over every stinkin' pipe I laid.

MANSON. I should make that a condition, comrade.

ROBERT [rising, he pulls off the cassock; goes to fire for his coat: returns: drags it on]. I don't know! Things 'av' got in a bit of a muck with me! I'm rather like a drain-pipe myself.

[With sudden inspiration]. There's one thing I *can* do!

MANSON. What's that?

ROBERT. Renahnce ole Beelzebub an' all 'is bloomin' wirks! 'And us that brarss-band!

> [He alludes to the ear-trumpet. MANSON obeying, ROBERT jabs it into the ear of the BISHOP, who seems quite surprised.]

'Ere! 'Av' you ever 'eard of 'ell?

BISHOP. Of what?

ROBERT. 'Ell. [Spelling.] H, E, double L, 'ell.

BISHOP. Well, my dear sir, I think I ought to!

ROBERT. Then, go there! Aymen . . . Now I'll go an' 'av' a look at our Bill's drains, damn 'is eyes!

> [He goes out through the main door, repentant.]

BISHOP. The scoundrel! Did you hear what he said? I shall certainly report him to his bishop!

MANSON. I don't think I should. *His* bishop doesn't mind a little plain speech now and again.

BISHOP. A little plain speech! Do you think it's right for a clergyman to—to direct me to perdition?

MANSON. I think you are making a mistake: the

MARY

man who gave you your—direction is not a clergy-man. He's a scavenger.

BISHOP. A scavenger!

MANSON. Yes—looks after drains.

BISHOP. Do you mean to tell me that I've been sitting down to breakfast with a common working-man?

MANSON. Yes; have you never done that before?

BISHOP. My dear sir, whatever do you take me for?

MANSON. A bishop of God's church.

BISHOP. Precisely! Is it *your* custom to break-fast with working-men?

MANSON. Every morning. You see, I'm prej-udiced: I was one myself, once.

BISHOP. You? . . .

MANSON. Yes—a long time ago, though: people have forgotten.

BISHOP. But, my dear brother, I am perfectly sure you never told people to go to . . .

MANSON. Oh yes, quite frequently: it would shock you to learn the language I really did use. Perhaps, under the circumstances, it might be ad-visable to drop the subject at this point.

BISHOP [emphatically]. I most certainly agree with you there! After all, it is a digression from the purpose for which we are here! . . .

[71]

Let me see, then: where were we? . . . Oh yes, I remember— Although, by the way, it was very ill-advised of you to speak your mind so openly in that man's presence! However . . .

To resume our—how shall I call it?—our—little understanding, eh?

MANSON. That describes it most accurately.

BISHOP. Now, you said, *Let's give as little, and grab as much as we can.* Of course, that is a playful way of putting it; but between ourselves, it expresses my sentiments exactly.

MANSON. I knew that when I said it.

BISHOP [delighted]. My dear brother, your comprehension makes my heart warm. I trust our relations may always remain as warm.

MANSON. Oh, warmer, warmer!

BISHOP. Very well then, to business! I tell you, candidly, I agree with you, that there is no necessity for sinking anything of our own in the concern: nothing ever comes of that sort of reckless generosity! If people want a church, let them make some sacrifice for it! Why should *we* do anything?

I am sure you will appreciate my candour?

MANSON. At its full value. Go on.

BISHOP. At the same time, there is no reason why we should throw cold water upon the project. On the contrary, we might promote it, encourage it, even lend it the influence of our patronage and our names. *But on one understanding!*

MANSON. And that?

BISHOP. That it is extended—imperialised, so to speak: that it is made the vehicle of a much vaster, of a much more momentous project behind it!

MANSON. You interest me intensely. Explain.

BISHOP. I will.

> [He looks around to assure himself
> that they are alone.]

There is in existence a society, a very influential society, in which I happen to have an interest—very great interest. Hm! I am one of the directors.

I may say that it is already very well established, financially; but it is always open to consider the—extension of its influence in that way.

MANSON. And the name of the society?

BISHOP. Rather long, but I trust explicit. It is called "*The Society for the Promotion and Preservation of Emoluments for the Higher Clergy.*"

MANSON. I do not seem to have heard it *named* before.

BISHOP. Well, no: its movements have always been characterised by a certain modesty. It is an invisible society, so to speak; but I can assure you its principles are very clearly understood—among the parties most concerned.

MANSON. And your project?

BISHOP. Affiliate the subsidiary question of the building of the Church, with the larger interests of the Society.

MANSON. Yes, but since people have already refused to subscribe to the more trivial project . . .

BISHOP. They have not been properly approached. My dear sir, in order to awaken public generosity, it is necessary to act like men of the world: *we must have names.* People will subscribe to any amount, if you can only get the right names.

That is where *you* come in.

MANSON. I! Do you propose to place *my* name at the head of your—prospectus?

BISHOP. My dear sir, invaluable! Didn't you say yourself that you brought in numberless millions, on your own credit, out there in India? Why shouldn't you do the same in England? Think of your reputation, your achievements, your name for sanctity— Not a word, sir: I *mean* it! . . . Why, there's no end to the amount it would bring in: it would mean billions!

Well, what do you say?

MANSON [slowly]. Let us clearly understand one

another.   I am to lend you my name—just my name —and you are to do all the rest.

BISHOP [quickly]. Oh yes: I'd *rather* you kept out of the business negotiations!

MANSON. It is rather a dangerous name to play with!

BISHOP. I take that responsibility entirely upon myself!

MANSON. And when all's over and done with, what are we going to gain out of the transaction?

BISHOP. We shall have to come to some private settlement between ourselves.

MANSON. When?

BISHOP. Oh, hereafter.

MANSON. Hereafter, then.

> [Enter AUNTIE and VICAR by door to right.]

AUNTIE [off]. Leave him to me, William! I'll soon settle the matter! [Entering.] The man must be possessed of some evil spirit! . . . Why—it's my brother James! . . .

> [MANSON has risen, and is now the butler once more. He speaks into the ear-trumpet.]

MANSON. Your sister and the vicar, my lord.

BISHOP [behind table, rising]. Ah! Well, Martha!
—No, no, no, if you please! [He restrains her ap-
proach.] Observe the retribution of an unchastened
will. You have never seen my face for sixteen years!
However, like a cloud, I blot out your transgressions
from this hour!

And so this is your husband?—Not a word, sir;
not a single word!—the sausages were delicious, and
your place has been most agreeably occupied by
your brother!

VICAR. My brother! Then you . . . What do
you mean?

BISHOP [testily]. I mean what I say, sir! Your
brother, *my* brother, *our* brother here, of course, our
Oriental brother!

AUNTIE. James, you are making a mistake: this
is our new butler—our *Indian* butler.

BISHOP. Your Indian—WHAT?

> [He stands cogitating horribly until
> the end of the act, facing towards
> MANSON.]

AUNTIE. What has made him like this? He seems
possessed!

MANSON. He is! . . .

I have just been having some trouble with *another*
devil, ma'am.

[76]

AUNTIE. Meaning, of course . . .
What has become of him?

MANSON [with his eye]. *He* is cast out forever.

AUNTIE. Where is he now?

MANSON. He walks through dry places seeking—
[he probes her soul]—*other* habitations.

AUNTIE. Manson! This is your doing! Oh, you
have saved us!

MANSON. I am trying to, ma'am; but, God knows,
you make it rather difficult!

> [A change comes over her face, as
> the curtain slowly falls.]

THE THIRD ACT

THE THIRD ACT

As the curtain rises, the scene and situation remain unchanged; but attention now centres in the Bishop, who appears to be struggling apoplectically for speech.

BISHOP [bursting]. Before we proceed a step further, I have a most extraordinary request to make! The fact is, you interrupted me in the middle of a most engrossing spiritual discussion with my . . . that is to say, with your . . . in short, *with that person standing over there!* My request is, that I be permitted a few minutes further conversation with him —alone, and at once!

ALL.   } With Manson! . . .
MANSON. } With me! . . .

BISHOP. Not a word! I know my request will appear singular—most singular! But I assure you it is most necessary. The peace, the security of a human soul depends upon it! Come, sir! Where shall we go?

MANSON. Have I your permission, ma'am?

AUNTIE. Certainly; but it is most extraordinary!

MANSON [crossing]. Then I think this way, my lord, in the drawing-room . . . [He leads the way.]

BISHOP [following]. And you may be sure, my good fellow, I will give anything—I say, anything—to remedy your misapprehensions! Hm!

> [They go into the drawing-room, right, MANSON holding the door for the other to pass.]

VICAR. Martha! It's no use! I can't do it!

AUNTIE [preoccupied]. Can't do what, William?

VICAR. Behave towards that man like a Christian! He stirs some nameless devil like murder in my heart! I want to clutch him by the throat, as I would some noisome beast, and strangle him!

AUNTIE [slowly]. He is greatly changed!

VICAR. It is you who have changed, Martha. You see him now with different eyes.

AUNTIE. Do I? I wonder! . . .

VICAR. After all, why should we invite him here? Why should we be civil to him? What possible kinship can there be between us? As for his filthy money—how did he scrape it together? How did he come by it? . . .

AUNTIE. Yes, William, that's true, but the opportunity of turning it to God's service . . .

VICAR. Do you think any blessing is going to

[82]

fall upon a church whose every stone is reeking with the bloody sweat and anguish of the human creatures whom the wealth of men like that has driven to despair? Shall we base God's altar in the bones of harlots, plaster it up with the slime of sweating-dens and slums, give it over for a gaming-table to the dice of gamblers and of thieves?

AUNTIE. Why will you exaggerate, my dear?— It is not as bad as that. Why don't you compose yourself and try and be contented and — and happy?

VICAR. How can I be happy, and that man poisoning the air I breathe?

AUNTIE. You are not always like this, dear! . . .

VICAR. Happy! How can I be happy, and my brother Robert what I have made him!

AUNTIE. We are not talking of Robert: we are talking of *you!* Think of our love, William—our great and beautiful love! Isn't that something to make you happy?

VICAR. Our love? It's well you mention it. That question had better be faced, too! Our love! Well, what of it? What is love?

AUNTIE. Oh, William, you *know* . . .

VICAR. Is love a murderer? Does love go roaming about the world like Satan, to slay men's souls?

[83]

AUNTIE. Oh, now you're exaggerating again! What do you mean?

VICAR. I mean my brother Robert! What has love done for him?

AUNTIE. Oh, Robert, Robert—I'm sick to death of Robert! Why can't you think of yourself?

VICAR. Well, I will! What has love done for *me*?

AUNTIE. William! . . .

> [The slightest pause. The scene takes on another complexion.]

VICAR. Do you remember that day when I first came to you and told you of my love? Did I lie to you? Did I try to hide things? Did I despise my birth? Did *you*?

AUNTIE. No, no, William, I loved you: I told you so.

VICAR. Did you mind the severance from your family because of me?

AUNTIE. Didn't I always say that I was proud to be able to give up so much for you, William? . . .

VICAR. Yes, and then what followed? Having given up so much for me, what followed?

AUNTIE. My dear, circumstances were too strong for us! Can't you see? *You* were not made to live out your life in any little odd hole and corner of

[84]

the world! There was your reputation, your fame:
you began to be known as an author, a scholar, a
wonderful preacher— All this required position,
influence, social prestige. You don't think I was
ambitious for myself: it was for *you*.

VICAR. For *me*—yes! And how do you imagine
I have benefited by all your scheming, your con-
triving, your compromising, your . . .

AUNTIE. In the way I willed! I am glad of it! I
worked for that—*and I won!* . . .

Well, what are you troubling about now?

VICAR [slowly]. I am thinking of the fact that there
has been no child to bless our marriage, Martha—
that is, no child of our very own, no child whose love
we have not stolen.

AUNTIE. My dear . . .

VICAR. We have spoken about it sometimes,
haven't we? Or, rather—*not* spoken!

AUNTIE. William, why will you think of these
things?

VICAR. In those first days, dearest, I brought you
two children of our own to cherish, little unborn
souls crying for you to mother them— You have
fostered only the one. That one is called the Scholar.
Shall I tell you the name of the other?

AUNTIE [after a moment]. Yes . . .

[85]

VICAR. I hardly know: I hardly dare to name him; but perhaps it was—the Saint.

AUNTIE. What I have done, William, has been done for love of you—you only—you only in the world!

VICAR. Yes: that's what I *mean!*

> [The thought troubles her for a moment: then she paces up and down in agitated rebellion.]

AUNTIE. No! I can't believe it! I can't think that love is as wrong as you say!

VICAR. Love is a spirit of many shapes and shadows: a spirit of fire and darkness—a minister of heaven and hell: Sometimes I think the very damned know love—in a way. It can inform men's souls with the gladness of high archangels, or possess them with the despair of devils!

> [She suddenly stands still, struck by the echo in his last phrase.]

Yes? . . .

AUNTIE. I was wondering . . .

Wondering what Manson meant just now.

VICAR. When?

AUNTIE. When he spoke about your brother Robert.

VICAR. I think he made it clear. He said we were—rid of him forever!

ROBERT

AUNTIE [thoughtfully]. Ye-es . . .
William, I begin to fear that man.

VICAR. Whom—Robert?

AUNTIE. No, Manson.

> [Re-enter MANSON from door, right.
> He carries a five-pound note in his
> hand.]

MANSON. His lordship will be glad to see you.

AUNTIE. Very well, Manson. Why, what have
you there?

MANSON. A remedy for misapprehension, ma'am.

AUNTIE. It's a five-pound note.

MANSON. Yes.

AUNTIE. Come, William.

> [She goes to the drawing-room door,
> her head anxiously turned towards
> MANSON.]

VICAR [at the door]. What are we going to do,
Martha?

AUNTIE. I don't know: God help me, I can't see
the way!

> [They both go out, MANSON watch-
> ing them. He then moves up to
> the fire, and burns the five-pound
> note. He watches the flames leap
> up as he speaks.]

[87]

MANSON. *Thou givest thy mouth to evil, and thy tongue frameth deceit. Thou sittest and speakest against thy brother: thou slanderest thine own mother's son. These things hast thou done, and I kept silence: thou thoughtest that I was altogether such an one as thyself: but I will reprove thee, and set them in order before thine eyes.*[1]

> [He comes down to the middle of the room. MARY enters eagerly. Seeing him alone, she gives a little cry of gladness.]

MARY. Oh, how jolly! Where are they?

MANSON. In the next room.

MARY. Ah! AH!

> [She comes to his out-stretched arms. He folds her to his heart, facing the audience.]

[Looking up into his face.] Isn't it a great secret? What shall I call you, now we are alone?

MANSON. Ssh! They may hear you!

MARY. If I whisper . . .

MANSON. They are very near! . . .

[Disengaging himself.] I must be about my business. Is this the bell to the kitchen?

[1] Psalms 1. 19–21

MARY. Yes.   Let me help you.

> [MANSON having rung the bell,
> they begin to remove the breakfast
> things.   MARY employs herself with
> the crumb-scoop.]

If auntie and uncle could see me now! If they only knew! I've kept the secret: I've told nobody!...

These will do for the birds. Look, I'll take them now. [She throws the crumbs out of the French windows.]   Poor little mites! [She returns to the table.]

MANSON. You are fond of the birds?

MARY. Just love them! Don't you?

MANSON. They are my very good friends.   Now, take the cassock.   Fold it up and put it on the chair.

> [ROGERS enters whilst he gives this
> command.]

ROGERS. Well, I'm . . .

'Owever, it's no business of mine!

MARY [brightly]. What's up with you, Rogers?

ROGERS [with reservation]. Nuthin', miss. [He fetches the tray.]

MARY. Then why look so solemn?

ROGERS [lugubriously]. Ain't lookin' solemn, miss.

MANSON. Hold up the tray, Rogers.

ROGERS. *Am* 'oldin' it up, Mr. Manson.

[89]

MARY [loading him up]. I'm sure there *is* something the matter!

ROGERS. Well, since you arsk me, miss, it's the goin's on in this 'ouse! I never see such a complicyted mass of mysteries and improbabilities in my life! I shall 'av' to give in my notice!

MARY. Oh, Rogers, that would be dreadful! Why?

MANSON. Now the cloth, Mary . . .

ROGERS. Cos why? *That's* why!—What you're doin' now! I likes people to keep their proper stytion! I was brought up middle-clarss myself, an' taught to be'ave myself before my betters!—No offence to *you*, Mr. Manson! [He says this with a jib, belying his words.]

MARY. Nonsense, Rogers! I like helping.

ROGERS. My poor farver taught me. 'E led a godly, righteous, an' sober life. 'E was a grocer.

MANSON. Come, Rogers. Take them to the kitchen.

> [ROGERS obeys with some asperity of mien. At the door he delivers a Parthian shot.]

ROGERS. If my poor farver could see what I've seen to-day, 'e would roll over in 'is grave!

> [MANSON opens the door for him. He goes.]

[90]

Mary [gayly]. Isn't he funny? Just because his silly old father . . .

Manson. Ssh! His father's *dead*, Mary!
[There is a sudden pause. He comes down to her.]
Well, have you thought any more about . . .

Mary. About wishing ?—Yes, lots.

Manson. And have you? . . .

Mary. I don't know what to think. You see, I never believed properly in wishing before. Wishing is a dreadfully difficult thing, when you *really* set about it, isn't it?

Manson. Yes.

Mary. You see, ordinary things won't do: they're all wrong, somehow. You'd feel a bit of a sneak to wish for *them*, wouldn't you?

Manson. Yes.

Mary. Even if you got them, you wouldn't care, after all. They'd all turn to dust and ashes in your hand.

That last bit is what Grannie Durden said.

Manson. Who's she?

Mary. She's the poor old woman I've been having breakfast with. Do you know, *she* said a funny thing about wishing. I must tell you first that she's quite blind and very deaf— Well, she's been wishing ever so long to see and hear; and at last she says she can!

MANSON. What—see and hear? [He glances towards the drawing-room.]

MARY. Um! I must say, I didn't notice any difference myself; but that's what she said.

She agreed with you, that wishing was the only way; and if you didn't know how, then you had to keep on wishing to wish, until you could.

MANSON. And so . . .

MARY. Well, that's as far as I've got.

[ROGERS re-enters.]

MANSON. Yes, what is it, Rogers?

ROGERS. Cook's compliments, Mr. Manson, and might she make so bold as to request your presence in the kitchen, seein' as she's 'ad no orders for lunch yet. O' course, she says, it will do when you've *quite* finished any private business you may 'av' in the upper part of the 'ouse!

[He delivers this with distinct hauteur. MANSON, smiling, goes up to him and takes his head in his hands.]

MANSON. Why do you dislike me so, Rogers?

ROGERS [taken aback]. Me? Me dislike you, Mr. Manson? *Oh no!*

MANSON. Come along, little comrade.

[They go out like brothers, MAN-
SON's arm round the lad's shoulders.]
[MARY is left seated on the table,
chuckling at the situation. Suddenly her face becomes serious
again: she is lost in thought. After
a while she speaks softly to herself.]

MARY. What have I needed most? What have
I not had?... Oh! I know!...

[Her face flames with the sudden
inspiration.]

And I never dreamed of it till now!

[ROBERT enters by the main door.
The child turns round, and, seeing
him, gives a startled little cry. They
stand facing each other, silent. Presently ROBERT falters.]

ROBERT. Beg pawdon, miss: I . . .

MARY. Who are you? What are you doing here?

ROBERT. I'm . . .
I was goin' ter see what's—what's in that room . . .

MARY. If you do, I'll . . .

[She moves swiftly to the bell.]

ROBERT. It's a mistake, miss. P'r'aps I'd—I'd
better tek my 'ook.

MARY. Stop! . . .

[93]

How dare you! Don't you know you're a very
wicked man?

ROBERT. Me, miss?

MARY. Yes, you.

ROBERT. Yus, I know it.

MARY [trying to save the sinner]. That isn't the
way to be happy, you know. Thieves are never
really happy in their hearts.

ROBERT. Wot's that? . . .

Do you tike me for a thief, miss? You? . . .

> [He advances to the table: she edges
> away.]

Why don't you arnser?

MARY. I had rather not say.

ROBERT. Cos why?

MARY. I don't want to be unkind.

> [ROBERT sinks stricken into the
> chair behind him.]

ROBERT. Oh, my Gawd, my Gawd!

MARY [relenting]. Of course, if—if you're sorry,
that makes a difference. Being sorry makes a lot
of difference. Doesn't it?

ROBERT. Yus, a fat lot!

MARY. Only you must never give way to such a
wicked temptation again. Oh, don't cry! [She goes
to him.]

[94]

ROBERT. Oo is cryin'? I'm not cryin'—not a cryin' sort! On'y—you 'adn't no right to talk to me like that, miss.

MARY. Why, didn't you own . . .

ROBERT. No, I didn't. It was you as jumped down my throat, an' took up my words afore I got 'em out.

MARY. Oh: I'm sorry. Did I make a mistake?

ROBERT. Yus, miss—a whopper.

MARY. Then you're not a . . .

ROBERT. *No*, swelp me Gaw— [He pulls himself up.] I assure you, no. I'm a bit of a low un; but I never come so stinkin' low as that.

You thought I looked like one, all the same. Didn't yer, now?

MARY. Well, you see, I thought you said so; and then there's your . . .

ROBERT. I know! You don't like my mug. It ain't much of a mug to look at, is it? Sort of a physog for a thief, eh? See them lines?—Want to know what them stand for? That's drink, an' starvytion, an' 'ard work, an' a damned lonely life.

MARY. Oh, you poor man!

ROBERT. Yus, miss, I am.

MARY. You mustn't say "damned," you know.

ROBERT. No, miss.

[95]

MARY. *That's* wicked, at any rate.

ROBERT. Yus, miss.

MARY. And you owned yourself that you drank. That's not very good, either.

ROBERT. No, miss.

MARY. So, you see, you *are* a little bit naughty, after all, aren't you?

ROBERT. Yus, miss.

MARY. Now, isn't it much nicer for you to try and look at things in this way? I'm sure you feel a great deal better already.

Do you know— Wait a moment . . .

> [She resumes her seat, turning it towards him, the passion of salvation in her eyes.]

Do you know, I'd like to do you some good!

ROBERT. You, miss?

MARY. Yes, wouldn't you like me to?

ROBERT. You're the on'y person in the world I'd—I'd like to see try, miss.

MARY [glad in the consciousness of "being used"]. That's because you know I'm interested in you, that I mean it, that I'm not trying to think only of myself.

ROBERT [a little stupidly]. Aren't you, miss?

MARY. No: we must always remember that there are other people in the world besides ourselves.

[This coincides with his experience: he says so.]

ROBERT. Yus, miss, there are.

MARY. Very well: now I'll see what I can do to help you.

ROBERT. Thank you, miss.

MARY. Now, don't you think, if you were really *to wish* very hard, it would make things better for you?

ROBERT. I don't know what you mean, miss.

MARY. Well, it's like this: if you only wish very very hard, everything comes true.

ROBERT. Wot *I* want, ain't no use wishing for!

MARY. It doesn't matter what it is! Anything you like! It will all happen!

ROBERT. Blimey, wot's the good o' talkin'?

MARY. Oh, wouldn't you like to help to spin the fairy-tale?

ROBERT [roughly]. I don't believe in no fairy-tales!

MARY. *I do!* I don't believe there's anything else in the world, if we only knew! And that's why I'm wishing! I'm wishing now! I'm wishing hard!

ROBERT [passionately]. So am I, Gawd 'elp me! But it's no use!

MARY. It is! It is! What are you wishing for?

ROBERT. Never you mind! Summat as impossible as—fairy-tales!

MARY. So's mine! That's what it has to be! Mine's the most impossible thing in the world!

ROBERT. Not more than mine!

MARY. What's yours?

ROBERT. What's yours?

MARY. *I want my father!*

ROBERT. I WANT MY LITTLE KID!

        [There is a second's pause.]

MARY. Your—what? . . .

ROBERT [brokenly]. My—daughter.

MARY. Oh! . . .

        [She goes towards him: they face each other.]

[Softly.] Is she dead?

        [He stands looking at her.]

Is she?

        [He turns away from her.]

ROBERT. Fur as I am concerned—yus.

MARY. What do you mean? *Isn't* she dead?

ROBERT. She's alive, right enough.

MARY. Perhaps—perhaps she ran away? . . .

ROBERT. She got took.

MARY. How do you mean—gypsies?

ROBERT. I *give* 'er up. 'Ad to.

MARY. Why?

ROBERT. Look at me! . . .

That—an' the drink, an' the low wages, an' my ole woman dyin'! That's why I give 'er up.

MARY. Where is she now?

ROBERT. Never you mind. She's bein' looked arfter.

MARY. By whom?

ROBERT. By people as I've allus 'ated like poison!

MARY. Why, aren't they kind to her?

ROBERT. Yus: they've made 'er summat, as I couldn't 'a' done.

MARY. Then why do you hate them?

ROBERT. I don't any longer. I 'ates myself, I 'ates the world I live in, I 'ates the bloomin' muck 'ole I've landed into!

MARY. Your wife's dead, you say?

ROBERT. Yus.

MARY. What would she think about it all?

ROBERT [hollowly, without variation]. I don't know: I don't know: I don't know.

[MARY sits down beside him.]

MARY [thoughtfully]. Isn't it strange—both our wishes alike! You want your little girl; and I, my father!

ROBERT. What sort of a . . .

[99]

MARY. Yes?

ROBERT. What sort of a bloke might your father be, miss?

MARY. I don't know. I have never seen him.

ROBERT. Got no idea? Never — 'eard *tell* of 'im?

MARY. Never.

ROBERT. 'Aven't thought of 'im yourself, I s'pose? Wasn't particular worth while, eh?

MARY. It's not that. I've been selfish. I never thought anything about him until to-day.

ROBERT. What made you think of 'im—to-day?

MARY. I can't quite say. At least . . .

ROBERT. Mebbe 'e wrote—sent a telingram or summat, eh?—t' say as 'e was comin'?

MARY [quickly]. Oh no: he never writes: we never hear from him. That's perhaps a bit selfish of him, too, isn't it?

ROBERT [after a moment]. Looks like it, don't it?

MARY. But I don't think he can be really selfish, after all.

ROBERT [with a ray of brightness]. Cos why?

MARY. Because he must be rather like my Uncle William and Uncle Joshua.

[He looks at her curiously.]

ROBERT. Like your . . .

[100]

MARY. Yes—they're his brothers, you know. This is Uncle William's house.

ROBERT. Yes, but what do you know about . . .

MARY. About Uncle Joshua? Well, I happen to know a good deal more than I can say. It's a secret.

ROBERT. S'pose your *Uncle William* spoke to you about *'im?*

MARY. Well, yes, Uncle William spoke about him, too.

ROBERT. But never about your father?

MARY. Oh no, never.

ROBERT. Why, miss?

MARY [slowly]. I—don't—know.

ROBERT. P'r'aps 'e ain't—good enough—to be— —to be the brother of your Uncle William—and—Uncle—Joshua—eh, miss?

MARY. Oh, I can't think that!

ROBERT. Why not, miss? Three good brothers in a family don't scarcely seem possible—not as families go—do they, miss?

MARY. You mustn't talk like that! A father must be much—much better than anybody else!

ROBERT. But s'pose, miss—s'pose 'e ain't . . .

MARY. He is! I know it! Why, that's what I'm wishing! . . .

ROBERT. P'r'aps it ain't altogether 'is fault, miss!...

MARY. Oh, don't! Don't . . .

ROBERT. Things may 'a' bin agin 'im, miss! . . .

MARY. Oh, you make me so unhappy! . . .

ROBERT. P'r'aps 'e's 'ad a 'ard life—a bitter 'ard life—same as I 'av', miss . . . [He breaks down.]

MARY. Ssh! Please! Please! . . .

I can quite understand: indeed, indeed, I can! I'm sorry—oh, so sorry for you. You are thinking of yourself and of your own little girl—the little girl who doesn't know what you have been telling me. Don't be miserable! I'm sure it will all turn out right in the end—things always do; far better than you dream! Only . . . don't take away *my* little dream!

> [She turns away her face. ROBERT rises heavily.]

ROBERT. All right, miss—I won't: swelp me Gawd, I won't. Don't cry, miss. Don't, miss! Breaks my 'eart—after all you've done for me. I ort never to 'a' bin born—mekin' you cry! Thank you kindly, miss: thank you very kindly. I'll—I'll tek my 'ook.

MARY. Oh, but I'm so sorry for *you!*

ROBERT. Thank you, miss.

MARY. I did so want to help you.

ROGERS

ROBERT. You 'av', miss.

MARY. Before you go, won't you tell me your name? Who are you?

ROBERT. I . . .

I got no name worth speakin' of, miss: I'm— just the bloke wot's a-lookin' arter the drains. Good-bye, miss.

> [At the door, he turns.]

Sorry I used bad words, miss.

> [She runs to him and offers her
> hand. He takes it.]

MARY. Good-bye.

ROBERT. Good-bye, miss.

> [He goes out.]
> [She shuts the door after him, and
> turns a wretched little face towards
> the audience as the curtain falls.]

THE FOURTH ACT

THE FOURTH ACT

As the curtain rises, the scene and situation remain unchanged. After a moment, Mary comes down to the settee,
left, and buries her face in the cushions, weeping. Shortly,
the handle of the drawing-room door is turned, and from
within there emerges a murmur of voices, the Vicar's
uppermost.

VICAR [within]. Very well, then, after you have
finished your letters! . . .

> [The voices continue confusedly:
> MARY rises quickly and goes into
> the garden.]
> [The VICAR enters and goes to the
> mantel-piece wearily: a moment
> later, AUNTIE.]

BISHOP [within]. I shall only be about twenty
minutes.

AUNTIE [entering]. All right, don't hurry, James:
you have all the morning.

> [She closes the door upon the BISH-
> OP'S grunts, and comes to the mid-
> dle of the room.]

[107]

VICAR. Hm! When he has finished his letters!

AUNTIE. Yes, things seem to be shaping better than we thought, William. Perhaps we have a little misjudged him.

[He looks at her curiously.]

To think, my dear, that the rebuilding of the church is becoming possible at last! All your hopes, all your enthusiasms, about to be realised! Now, it only remains to gain your brother Joshua's approval and help, and the scheme is complete!

VICAR. Supposing he — doesn't approve of the scheme?

AUNTIE. My dear, he must approve: he will see the advantages at once. I think James made that perfectly clear! . . .

And then, look at the opportunities it creates for *you!* Not only the church, William, the beautiful big church of your dreams, with the great spires and flashing crosses and glorious windows; but a much larger sphere of usefulness than you ever dared to dream! Think of your work, William, of your great gifts—even James had to acknowledge them, didn't he?—Think of the influence for good you will be able to wield! Ah! And then I shall see my beloved, *himself* again — No more worry, no more feverish nights and days, none of the wretched frets and fancies that have been troubling him all this morning; but the great Scholar and Saint again, the master of men's souls, the priest in the congregation!

VICAR. Suppose you try and forget me for a moment. Do you think you can?

AUNTIE. William, that's unkind! Of course I can't.

VICAR. It might mean the salvation of my soul.

AUNTIE. Oh, William! Now you're going to begin to worry again!

VICAR. Oh no: I'm quite calm. Your brother's powers of reasoning have left me philosophical. . . .

Tell me, are you quite sure that you have grasped the full meaning of his project?

AUNTIE. Of course! You think no one can understand a simple business dealing but men! Women are every bit as clever!

VICAR. Well, then, this project: what was it?

AUNTIE. James explained clearly enough: the affiliation of your brother's scheme with that of the society he mentioned.

VICAR. Yes—*what* society?

AUNTIE. *The Society for the Extension of Greater Usefulness among the Clergy.* . . . It was an admirable suggestion—one that ought to appeal particularly to you. Haven't you always said, yourself, that if only you had enough money to . . .

VICAR. Did you happen to realise his explanation as to the constitution of the society?

AUNTIE. To tell the truth, I wasn't listening just then: I was thinking of you.

VICAR. The *financial* possibilities of the scheme— Did his eloquence on that point escape you?

AUNTIE. Figures always bore me, and James uses dreadfully long words.

VICAR. Did you hear nothing of *profits?*

AUNTIE. I only heard him say that you were to . . .

VICAR. Well, didn't it strike you that throughout the entire discussion he spoke rather like a *tradesman?*

AUNTIE. My dear, you can't expect everybody to be an idealist! Remember, he's a practical man: he's a bishop.

VICAR. Didn't it strike you that there are some things in this world which are not to be bought at *any* price?

AUNTIE. My dear William, bricks and mortar require money: you can't run a society without funds!

VICAR. Yes, but what of flesh and blood? What of reputation? What of a man's name?

AUNTIE. Whatever do you mean now?

VICAR. Didn't his proposal practically amount to this: that we should turn my brother Joshua's name and reputation into a bogus Building Society, of which the funds were to be scraped together from all the naked bodies and the starving bellies of the world, whilst *we* and our thieving co-directors should collar all the swag?

AUNTIE. Now, that's exactly where I think you are so unjust! Didn't you yourself refuse, before he spoke a word, to let him put a penny of his own into the concern? I must say, you were unnecessarily rude to him about that, William!

VICAR. Yes, and didn't he jump at the suggestion!

AUNTIE. He offers to give his patronage, his influence, his time. All he asks of your brother is his bare name.

VICAR. Yes, and all he asks of me is simply my eloquence, my gift of words, my power of lying plausibly!

AUNTIE. William, he is offering you the opportunity of your life!

VICAR. Damnation take my life!

AUNTIE. William, why are you so violent?

VICAR. Because violence is the only way of coming to the truth between you and me!

AUNTIE [now thoroughly afraid]. What do you mean by the truth, William?

VICAR. I mean this: What is the building of this church to you? Are you so mightily interested in architecture, in clerical *usefulness*, in the furtherance of God's work?

AUNTIE. I am interested in *your* work, William. Do you take me for an atheist?

VICAR. No: far worse—for an idolater!

AUNTIE. William . . .

VICAR. What else but idolatry is this precious husband-worship you have set up in your heart— you and all the women of your kind? You barter away your own souls in the service of it: you build up your idols in the fashion of your own respectable desires: you struggle silently amongst yourselves, one against another, to push your own god foremost in the miserable little pantheon of prigs and hypocrites you have created!

AUNTIE [roused]. It is for your own good we do it!

VICAR. Our own good! What have you made of me? You have plucked me down from whatever native godhead I had by gift of heaven, and hewed and hacked me into the semblance of your own idolatrous imagination! By God, it shall go on no

[112]

longer! If you have made me less than a man, at least I will prove myself to be a priest!

AUNTIE. Do you call it a priest's work to . . .

VICAR. It is *my* work to deliver you and me from the bondage of lies! Can't you see, woman, that God and Mammon are about us, fighting for our souls?

AUNTIE [determinedly]. Listen to me, William, listen to me . . .

VICAR. I have listened to you too long!

AUNTIE. You would always take my counsel before . . .

VICAR. All that is done with! I am resolved to be a free man from this hour—free of lies, free of love if needs be, free even of you, free of everything that clogs and hinders me in the work I have to do! I will do my own deed, not yours!

AUNTIE [with deadly quietness]. If I were not certain of one thing, I could never forgive you for those cruel words: William, this is some madness of sin that has seized you: it is the temptation of the devil!

VICAR. It is the call of God!

AUNTIE [still calmly]. That's blasphemy, William! But I will save you—yes, I will—in spite of yourself. I am stronger than you.

[113]

[They look at each other steadily for a moment, neither yielding.]

VICAR. Then I accept the challenge! It is God and I against you, Martha!

AUNTIE. God and I against *you*, William.

VICAR. So now—for my work!

AUNTIE [quietly]. Yes : what are you going to do ?

VICAR. Three things.

AUNTIE. Yes—and they ? . . .

VICAR. Tell Mary everything: send for my brother, Robert: and then — answer that monster in there.

AUNTIE [fearfully]. William, you would never dare! . . .

VICAR. Look! . . .

[MARY re-enters from the garden.]

MARY. Auntie! Uncle! I want to speak to you at once—both of you!

VICAR. You are just in time: I wanted to speak to *you* at once.

MARY. Is it important, uncle ? Mine's dreadfully important.

VICAR. So is mine.

AUNTIE [quickly]. Let the child speak, William. Perhaps . . .

[114]

MARY. I hardly know how to begin.   Perhaps it's only my cowardice.   Perhaps it isn't really dreadful, after all . . .

AUNTIE [troubled]. Why, what are you thinking of, Mary?

MARY. It's about something we have never spoken of before; something I've never been told.

VICAR [searchingly]. Yes? . . .

AUNTIE [falteringly]. Yes? . . .

MARY. I want to know about my father.

> [There is a short silence.   The
> VICAR looks at AUNTIE.]

VICAR. Now: is God with you or me, Martha?

MARY. What do you mean by that?   Is it very terrible, uncle?

> [He stands silent, troubled.   MARY
> crosses him, going to AUNTIE.]

Auntie . . .

AUNTIE. Don't ask me, child: I have nothing to tell you about your father.

MARY. Why, isn't he . . .

AUNTIE. I have nothing to tell you.

VICAR. I have.

AUNTIE. William! . . .

VICAR. I have, I say!   Come, sit here, Mary.

> [She sits to left of him, on the settee.

AUNTIE is down stage on the other side of him.]

Now! What do you want to know about your father?

MARY [passionately]. Everything there is to know!

AUNTIE. William, this is brutal! . . .

VICAR. It is *my work*, Martha!—God's work! Haven't I babbled in the pulpit long enough about fatherhood and brotherhood, that I should shirk His irony when He takes me at my word!

Now: what put this thought into your head to-day?

MARY. I don't know. I've been puzzling about something all the morning; but there was nothing clear. It only came clear a few minutes ago—just before I went into the garden. But I think it must have begun quite early—before breakfast, when I was talking to my—to Manson.

AUNTIE. Manson! . . .

MARY. And then, all of a sudden, as I was sitting there by the fireplace, *it came*—all in a flash, you understand! I found myself wishing for my father: wondering why I had never seen him: despising myself that I had never thought of him before.

VICAR. Well, what then?

MARY. I tried to picture him to myself. I imagined all that he must be. I thought of you, Uncle

[116]

William, and Uncle Joshua, and of all the good and noble men I had ever seen or heard of in my life; but still—that wasn't quite like a father, was it? I thought a father must be much, much better than anything else in the world! He must be brave, he must be beautiful, he must be good! I kept on saying it over and over to myself like a little song: he must be brave, he must be beautiful, he must be good! [Anxiously.] That's true of fathers, isn't it, uncle? Isn't it?

VICAR. A father ought to be all these things.

MARY. And then . . . then . . .

VICAR. Yes? . . .

MARY. I met a man, a poor miserable man—it still seems like a dream, the way I met him—and he said something dreadful to me, something that hurt me terribly. He seemed to think that my father— that perhaps my father—might be nothing of the sort!

AUNTIE. Why, who was he—the man?

MARY. He wouldn't tell me his name: I mistook him for a thief at first; but afterwards I felt very, very sorry for him. You see, his case was rather like my own. *He was wishing for his little girl.*

[There is a short silence.]

VICAR. Where did you meet with him?

MARY. Here, in this room.

AUNTIE. When was this?

MARY. A few minutes ago—just before you came in.

AUNTIE. Where is he now?

MARY. He said good-bye. He has gone away.

AUNTIE. For good?

MARY. Yes, I think so: I understood him to mean that.

VICAR. Was he—a rough-looking man?

MARY. Dreadfully; and he swore once—but afterwards he said he was sorry for that.

VICAR. Did he frighten you at all?

MARY. No, not exactly frighten: you see, I felt sorry for him.

VICAR [slowly]. *And he wouldn't tell you his name?* . . .

MARY. No: I asked him, but he wouldn't.

> [The VICAR ponders this for a moment.]

AUNTIE. Now, is it God with you or with me, William?

> [For a moment this unnerves him. Then setting his teeth together, he faces his task stubbornly.]

VICAR. Have you any idea about this man?

MARY. How do you mean—any idea?

VICAR. As to why he put this doubt into your head about your father.

MARY. He seemed to be thinking about himself, and how unworthy he was of his own little girl.

VICAR. Did *he* say—unworthy?

MARY. That's what I think he meant. What he said was that perhaps my father wasn't good enough to be your brother, uncle. That's not true, is it?

VICAR. No, by Heaven! *That's not true!*

MARY [rapturously]. Oh, I knew it, I knew it!

VICAR [in an agony]. Stop! You don't understand!

MARY. I understand quite enough! That's all I wanted to know!

VICAR. Listen, child! Listen! I mean that it is I who am not worthy to be called his brother.

AUNTIE. William, this is absurd!

MARY [snuggling up to him]. Isn't he a dear?

VICAR [freeing himself]. Listen to me, Mary: I have something awful to tell you: try and bear it bravely. You will hate me for it—never love me again! . . . No, listen! . . .

Supposing your father were—not what you imagine him to be? . . .

MARY. Uncle, didn't you just say . . .

VICAR. Supposing that wretched man you spoke with just now were right, after all! What would you say?

MARY. Uncle! . . .

VICAR. Supposing he were one upon whom all the curses of the world had been most cruelly visited —his poor body scarred and graven out of human semblance; his soul the prey of hate and bitterness; his immortal spirit tortured and twisted away from every memory of God! What would you say?

MARY. Uncle, it would be terrible—terrible!

VICAR. What will you say, then, to the man who has brought him to such ruin? What will you say to that man being God's priest? What word of loathing have you for the thief who has stolen the love of another man's child, for the murderer who has slain his brother's soul?

MARY. Uncle, do you mean . . . do you mean . . .

VICAR. I mean that I am the man!

MARY. You! . . .

AUNTIE [passionately]. It is not true! It is a lie! It's entirely your father's own fault!

MARY. I don't understand. Why should Uncle William lie to me?

AUNTIE. He is overwrought: he is ill. It is like

[120]

your uncle William to take upon himself another man's wickedness!

MARY. Then, *that* is true, at least: my father is a *wicked* man! . . .

AUNTIE. I don't want to speak about your father!

MARY. He is nothing that I have wished him to be: not *brave* . . .

VICAR. Yes—*that* at least!

MARY [turning towards him]. *Beautiful?* . . .

VICAR. What do you mean by beautiful?

MARY. You know what I mean: What you once said God was, when you called *Him* beautiful.

VICAR. I have no right to judge your father.

[She perceives the evasion.]

MARY. Not even—*good?* . . .

VICAR. He is what I have made him. I and no other!

[She stands looking at him piteously.]

AUNTIE. There is another—I! I kept them apart: I poisoned your uncle against him: I took you away from him: it was I who kept you in ignorance of your father!

MARY. Why? . . .

AUNTIE. Because he stands in the way of my husband's happiness! Because, even, he is your father! Because I hate him! I could almost *wish him dead!*

VICAR. Martha! . . .

[There is a long pause.]

MARY. Then I have nobody, now. It's no use wishing any more.

AUNTIE. Mary . . .

MARY. No! . . . I want to be alone.

> [She goes out into the garden. They follow her out with their eyes.]

VICAR. So! God has revealed His partisanship!— He has beggared us both!

> [AUNTIE considers this for a moment. Then, with sudden determination, she rises.]

AUNTIE. I am not going to be beggared without a struggle for it, William!

> [She moves briskly across to the bell.]

VICAR. What are you going to do, Martha?

AUNTIE. [flashing round passionately, before she can ring the bell]. Do you think I am going to stand by and see your life wrecked—yours and that child's?

VICAR. We are not the only persons concerned, Martha.

AUNTIE. As far as I care, you are!

VICAR. And what of Robert? . . .

AUNTIE. Robert! That's what I'm going to see to now!

[She rings the bell.]

There's only one way of dealing with a brute like that!

VICAR. What's that?

AUNTIE. Pack him off to Australia, Africa—anywhere, so long as we are never pestered with him again!

VICAR. Do you think you'll get him to go?

AUNTIE. Oh, I'll find the money! A drunkard like that will do anything for money! Well, he shall have plenty: perhaps he'll drink himself to . . .

VICAR. By Heaven, but I say no!

AUNTIE. By Heaven, but I say yes! It's about time I took things in hand again! Do you think I'm going to risk that child learning everything? She knows more than enough already! Providentially, she does not know the worst!

VICAR. And what knowledge do you consider Providence has so kindly spared her?

AUNTIE. The knowledge *who that man was!* She shall never know, if I can have my way! [She rings the bell again, impatiently.] Why doesn't he come? Why doesn't he come?

VICAR. Who?

AUNTIE. Manson.

[Enter MANSON by the main door.

> There is a subtle change in the man-
> ner of him, a look in his eye, as of
> the servant merging in the master.]

MANSON. You rang.

AUNTIE. Yes, come in, Manson. I want to have a little confidential talk with you—confidential, you understand.

MANSON [eying her]. If you please. I expected this.

> [He has the air of a judge. She
> hurries on, unheeding.]

AUNTIE. Manson, you saw everything. You were here when that dreadful creature arrived.

MANSON. Which?

AUNTIE. Why, my husband's brother, Robert. Didn't you tell me, William, that Manson heard everything he said?

VICAR. Yes.

AUNTIE. Then you will know the wretched plight we are in. Manson, it's terrible. I want your help. By-the-way, you have not spoken about it to the other servants?

MANSON. I am always most discreet.

AUNTIE [touched]. Thank you, Manson, thank you: I felt that I could trust you. It's to prove my trust that I've sent for you now. Perhaps I'd better begin by explaining everything quite clearly, so that you . . .

MANSON. There is no need. I know everything already.

AUNTIE. Everything! How? . . .

MANSON. A certain gift of divination—mine by birth. And, besides, you forget that I had a long conversation with your brother-in-law after master left the room.

AUNTIE. What! Whilst my brother was here?

MANSON. Yes: we all three had breakfast together.

AUNTIE. Breakfast together! Then James has heard all!

MANSON. Not quite all. You may have observed that your brother is a little deaf.

AUNTIE. But surely— What did he think?

MANSON. He mistook him for your husband.

AUNTIE. My husband!

MANSON. Your brother is also a little blind, remember.

AUNTIE [delighted]. Then James never found out? . . .

MANSON. Oh yes: I took care to undeceive him on the point.

AUNTIE. Good gracious! How did he take it?

MANSON. At first, a little angrily; but, after a while,

some few poor words of my own chanced to move him to more—*profitable* meditation.

AUNTIE. Manson, you're perfectly wonderful! I respect you very, very much!

MANSON. It is not enough. I shall require more.

AUNTIE [embarrassed]. Oh, of course, I shall be glad to do anything that . . .

Why, what do you mean? . . .

MANSON. I mean that service such as mine demands a greater recompense!

AUNTIE. You may be sure that anything in reason . . .

MANSON. It must go beyond that!

AUNTIE. Well, what do you ask?

MANSON. The uttermost obedience, loyalty, and love!

AUNTIE. Manson, how dare you! By what right . . .

MANSON. By my own right!

AUNTIE. This is insolence! What right do you mean?

MANSON. The right of understanding, the right of purpose, and the right of will!

AUNTIE. You force me to speak angrily to you! Do you forget that you are my servant?

THE SERVANT IN THE HOUSE. ACT IV.

MANSON. No! And, therefore, it is my office to command you now!

Sit down, and hear me speak!

VICAR. He has been sent to help us! Martha, this is God!

MANSON. Over here, please. [He points to the settee.]

AUNTIE. I . . . I . . .

> [MANSON still points. She wavers as in a dream, and at length moves mechanically across the room, obeying him.]

MANSON. Now, let me tell you exactly why you have sent for me here. There is a strange and wretched turmoil in your soul: you have done wrong, and you know it—but you don't know all! You would keep what miserable little right you have by bolstering it up with further wrong. And you have sent for me to help you in that wrong!

AUNTIE. How dare you say that?

MANSON. Haven't you sent for me to help you in your plans about his brother, Robert?

AUNTIE [faintly]. What plans? . . .

MANSON. The plan of banishing him further from your lives than ever! The plan of *providing* for him! The plan of patching up his bitter wrongs with gold!

AUNTIE. How did you know that?

MANSON. I know *you!* What, do you think that God's eyes are like your brother's—blind? Or do you think these things can be done in darkness without crying aloud to Heaven for light?

AUNTIE. I am here to work my will, not yours!

MANSON. What gain do you hope to bring yourself by that?

AUNTIE. I am not thinking of myself! I am thinking only of my husband's happiness!

MANSON. Behold the happiness you have already brought him!

AUNTIE. There is the child! It would break her heart!

MANSON. What is her heart but broken now—by you?

AUNTIE. Robert himself would be the first to repudiate any other plan.

MANSON. Have you tried him?

AUNTIE. Of course not; but he must see the impossibility.

MANSON. What impossibility?

AUNTIE. The impossibility of having him here: the impossibility of letting him see the child: the impossibility of him and his brother ever meeting again!

MANSON. Is that your only difficulty?

AUNTIE. Only difficulty! What, would you have me welcome him with open arms?

MANSON. Yes, and heart, too!

AUNTIE. Have him here, entertain him, treat him as a guest?

MANSON. As an honoured guest!

AUNTIE. In this house?

MANSON. This house.

AUNTIE. Good Heavens! what else?

MANSON. Sweep and garnish it throughout, seek out and cleanse its hidden corners, make it fair and ready to lodge him royally as a brother!

AUNTIE [desperately]. I won't do it! I can't! I can't!

MANSON. With my assistance, you can!

VICAR. Manson, how can we bring it about?

AUNTIE. I daren't! I daren't!

VICAR. I dare! I will!

AUNTIE. In God's name, how is it possible?

MANSON. *Make me the lord and master of this house for one little hour!*

VICAR. By Heaven, yes!

MANSON. And you? You? . . .

> [She falters a few moments: then,
> utterly broken down, she whispers,
> feebly.]

AUNTIE. Yes.

MANSON. Then first TO CLEANSE IT OF ITS ABOMI-
NATIONS!

> [The BISHOP enters from the draw-
> ing-room.   He carries a letter in his
> hand.]

BISHOP. Well, here is the letter I have written to
the secretary of our Society: I have explained everything quite nicely; and have warned him, of course,
against doing anything definite in the matter until
we have consulted your dear brother.   Now . . .
Eh, what?   Oh! . . .

> [MANSON has tapped his ear, per-
> emptorily: he fixes his ear-trumpet.]

MANSON. I bear you a message from the master
of this house.   Leave it.

BISHOP. Really, I . . . . Most extraordinary!
Hm!

> [He blows down the ear-trumpet,
> and afterwards wipes it very care-
> fully with his handkerchief.   MAN-
> SON stands, as though carven in mar-
> ble, waiting for him to fix it again.]

Now: again, please.

MANSON. You are no longer necessary.   Leave
this house.

BISHOP. You scoundrel! You impudent scoundrel! You . . . You . . .

Give me back my five-pound note!

MANSON [pointing to the fire]. It is invested for you.

BISHOP. I will have it back at once!

MANSON. Hereafter, was the arrangement.

BISHOP. Mr. Smythe! Where are you? Do you hear what this blackguard says?

VICAR. I endorse it, every word.

BISHOP. Martha! . . .

> [She turns away from him as from some horror of sin. The BISHOP stands dumfounded for a moment or two: then he boils over.]

Now I see it all! I've been trapped, I've been tricked! Martha, this is all your doing! Brought me here on a trumped-up story of relationship with the Bishop of Benares, to insult me! Oh, what would that godly man say if he heard of it!—And he *shall* hear of it, believe me! Your infamy shall be spread abroad! So this is your revenge, sir—[he turns to the VICAR]—your revenge for the contumely with which I have very properly treated you, sir! *Now* I understand why I was made to sit down and eat sausages with a butler—yes, sir, with a butler and a common working-man! Oh! I could die with shame! You have bereft me of all words! You... You... You are no scholar, sir! And your Greek is contemptible!...

[He crosses to AUNTIE.] Martha! You are no sister of mine henceforward! [Going, he returns to her.] Anathema maranatha!

> [He bounces up to the door, but
> turns back again for a last word with
> MANSON.]

And I have one word for you, sir! You are a scoundrel, sir—a cheat, an impostor! And if I could have my way with you, I would have you publicly whipped: I would visit you with the utmost rigour of the law: I would nail you up, sir, for an example!

MANSON. I have encountered similar hostility before, my lord—from gentlemen very like your lordship. Allow me . . .

> [He opens the door, his eyes flash-
> ing.]

BISHOP. Don't trouble, sir. I can get my hat and my stick and my portmanteau for myself! I can do very well without *your* assistance—thank God!

> [He stumps out. MANSON closes the
> door after him, barring it, as it were,
> with his great left arm. He lifts

the other arm slowly, as commanding silence. After a moment the front door is heard slamming noisily.] [AUNTIE sinks, weeping, upon the settee. The VICAR goes over to comfort her. The uplifted hand of MANSON assumes the BISHOP's sign of blessing as the curtain slowly falls.]

THE FIFTH ACT

THE FIFTH ACT

As the curtain rises, the scene and situation remain unchanged.

> [There is heard a Ring of the Bell.
> All three turn their heads, alert.]

VICAR. If it's my brother . . .

MANSON. Which?

VICAR. I meant—the Bishop of Benares; but . . .

AUNTIE [hand on his arm, apprehensively]. William . . .

MANSON. It wants ten minutes of the time you said you expected him. [Goes to door: turns.] Only ten minutes.

> [He goes out, closing the door
> softly.]

VICAR. Ten minutes! . . .

AUNTIE. We shall never be able to do it, William! How can we possibly undo the work of all these years in ten minutes? It wants a miracle.

VICAR. We must make the attempt, somehow.

AUNTIE. Yes—yes: how? Oh, I have been blind

[137]

—blind! [She walks across the room in agitation.] Where has he gone, I wonder? We don't even know that—where he is!

VICAR [making a movement]. Perhaps Manson . . .

AUNTIE. No, no, no: it must be ourselves . . .

Ten minutes!—And no assistance on *his* side: we can't expect it, after our treatment of him. He will hate *me* most of all: there's the chief difficulty! . . .

VICAR. You would say *me*, if you had seen his face and heard his voice this morning!

AUNTIE. God help us, God pity us!

VICAR. Amen . . .

Then, there's the child, too! That difficulty must be faced.

AUNTIE. Yes—no escape! We shall have to pay the whole debt, William: I see that.

VICAR. Who knows! Perhaps the child will have to pay most, when all is done.

AUNTIE. The innocent for the guilty—yes . . . Oh, William, William, can you ever forgive me?

VICAR. There is much to forgive, both sides, Martha. My sin has been greater than yours. You have only loved unworthily in blindness: I have seen clearly and been a coward.

[Enter MARY from the garden.]

Mary! . . .

MARY. Let me speak, uncle. I have been thinking, out there in the garden—thinking very hard: I've been trying to put things together again and make them straight; but it's still very difficult. Only there's one thing—I'm sorry I was unkind just now: I didn't mean it: you are everything I have—everything I have ever had; and as for what uncle said—about himself, I mean—I can't believe it. No, I'm sure there's a mistake somewhere; and mistakes can always be put right, if we only help one another and mean it. Shall we try, uncle? Shall we, auntie?

AUNTIE. If it's not too late! . . .

MARY. It can't be too late, auntie dear, if we all wish very hard. I was a coward to give up wishing. That was *my* sin, too!

AUNTIE. God knows, I wish, Mary! . . .

VICAR. And I! . . .

MARY. And, indeed, I do! . . .

Now, I've been thinking: I've been trying to look the worst in the face. Supposing my father *is* the wicked man you say—the very, very wickedest man that ever lived, don't you think if we tried to love him very much it might make a difference?

VICAR. What made you think of that, Mary? . . .

MARY [simply]. It's what you taught me, uncle, in your sermons.

[139]

VICAR. *I* taught you? . . .

MARY. Yes: and, besides, there's another reason . . . I've been thinking of the poor man I met this morning.

AUNTIE. ⎱ Yes . . .
VICAR. ⎰ What of him? . . .

MARY. *He* said he was a wicked man, and at first he looked so dreadfully wicked, I believed him; but when I began to look at him closely, and heard him talk about his little girl, everything seemed different! I could no more believe him, than I can believe you, uncle, when you say such awful things about yourself! I believe he was a much better man than he ever dreamed! And so I think we might find my father just the same, if he was properly loved and looked after!

VICAR [with determination]. Then listen to me, Mary: I have something to tell you: that very man you spoke to . . .

　　　　　　[ROGERS enters, his face betraying
　　　　　　signs of his morning's affliction.]

ROGERS. Beg your pardon, sir; but . . .

VICAR. Yes, Rogers: what is it?

ROGERS. Mr. Manson sent me, sir; it ain't my fault! . . .

VICAR. Do explain yourself, Rogers!

ROGERS. Well, sir, it's a bit orkard: it's . . . I really don't know what you'll say, sir, I don't really . . .

VICAR [impatiently]. Come, come, come, what is it?

ROGERS. *It's a man, sir!*

VICAR. Well, there's nothing very extraordinary in that. Wants to see me, eh?

ROGERS. Yes, sir; and what's more, Mr. Manson told me to *bring 'im in!*

VICAR. Well, why don't you?

ROGERS. 'E's mucked up to the eyes, sir! Bin down the drains! *It's the same chap as come an' made so free 'ere this mornin'!*

[There is a general rapturous excitement.]

VICAR. Praise God! Shew him in at once!

ROGERS [flabbergasted]. What! In *'ere,* sir? . . .

VICAR. Come, come, come!

[ROGERS's cosmos is fast slipping away: he crawls abjectly to the door: his hand on the knob, he turns once more a face of bewildered inquiry upon the VICAR, who snaps his fingers impatiently.]

ROGERS [with a sickly smile]. 'E's just outside, sir.

[*Opening the door, he whines.*]
Oh, *do* come in.

[ROBERT *enters, amply fulfilling the
lad's description. The latter lags
out, nauseated with the world.*]

[ROBERT *stands up stage, in the
middle:* AUNTIE *and* VICAR, *down
stage, one on either side.* MARY
with her aunt.]

ROBERT. Can I be 'eard civil in this 'ouse, if I
speak a few words?

[*They make a movement as towards
him.*]

'Old back! Don't you come near me! Don't
you so much as speak till I've done!...

[*To Auntie and Vicar respectively*]. You don't
know me: *you* don't know me ... Understand?

There's no one 'ere as knows oo I am, excep' one
little gel—'*er* over there. Now, keep quiet! 'Ere!...

[MARY *goes up to him.*]

Tell 'em oo I am.

MARY. Why, it's my friend—the man I was telling you about! The man who looks after the drains!

ROBERT. That's about it: I'm the drain-man,
see? Thought you might be mistakin' me for—
summat else, if you wasn't told. Now you know.

[MARY's face, as she returns, bears the first dawn of an idea. The VICAR lifts a hand of warning to AUNTIE.]

VICAR. Go on.

ROBERT. That's what I come 'ere to talk abaht—my job. P'r'aps you'll think as it ain't a tasty subjic, before a lot o' nice, clean, respectable people as never 'ad anythin' worse on their fingers than a bit of lawn-dirt, playin' crokey; but *some one* 'as to see to the drains, *some one* 'as to clear up the muck of the world! I'm the one.

An' I'm 'ere to tell you about it.

AUNTIE [involuntarily]. Oh! . . .

ROBERT. You don't like that, ma'am? 'Urts your feelin's, eh?

AUNTIE. Yes; but not in the way you mean.

MARY. But you know, you really are a little unpleasant!

ROBERT. I'm not 'ere to be pleasant, young leddy: I'm 'ere to edicate you.

VICAR. Yes, I think I see!

AUNTIE [breathlessly]. Go on: go on!

ROBERT. Well, I come to this 'ouse this mornin', I don't mind ownin' it, in a rotten bad frame of mind; I 'ad a little job on 'and—a job a bit above my 'ead, an' it got me dahn an' worried me: yus it did—worried me. That young leddy 'll tell you wot I was like when *she* fust saw me: I looked that bad, she thought I come to steal summat! Well, p'r'aps I did, arter all—summat as I 'ad no right to, summat as don't properly belong to a streaky swine like me. That was when *she* fust saw me; but I was wuss before that, I tell you strite!

MARY [self-consciously]. What changed you?

ROBERT. A bloke I met, miss, as knowed me better than I knowed myself. 'E changed me.

AUNTIE. ⎫ Manson! . . .
VICAR. ⎬ Manson! . . .
MARY. ⎭ Oh, I thought, perhaps . . .

ROBERT. Don't know 'is name; 'e was a fair knock-aht— Got togs on 'im like an Earl's Court Exhibition . . . '*E* changed me: 'e taught me my own mind; 'e brought me back to my own job—*drains*.

AUNTIE. Yes . . .

ROBERT. Funny thing, ma'am, people's born different: some's born without noses in their 'eads, worth speakin' of. I wasn't—I can smell out a stink anywhere.

AUNTIE [fascinated]. I am sure you can. This is most interesting!

ROBERT [warming]. Moment I stuck my 'ead in

this 'ouse, I knowed as summat was wrong in my line, and I ses to myself: *Wot oh, 'e ain't such an awlmighty liar, arter all—that's drains!* An' drains it was, strike me dead—arskin' your pawdon!

MARY. Now, didn't I always say . . .

ROBERT. Yus, miss, you're one o' the nosey uns, I can see! Well, soon as ole Togs got done with 'is talk, I got my smeller dahn, follered up the scent, an' afore I knowed where I was, I was in it, up to my eyes!—Out there in the room with the blood-red 'eap o' books! Blimey, you never did see! Muck, ma'am!—Just look at my 'ands! Ain't that pretty?

'Owever, I got there, right enough, I don't fink! Fancy I put that little bit strite afore I done!

AUNTIE. Oh, this is too beautiful of you! . . .

ROBERT [burning with enthusiasm, and manifestly affected by her appreciation]. Wait a bit: I got more yet! Talk abaht bee-utiful!—That bit was on'y an ash-pan! Look 'ere, ma'am, I got the loveliest little job on as ever yer soiled yer 'ands in! . . .

MARY. Oh, do tell us! . . .

AUNTIE. } Yes, do! . . .
VICAR. } Yes, yes! . . .

> [A splendid rapture infects them all.]

ROBERT. I followed up that drain—*I* wasn't goin'

to stick till kingdom come inside your little mouse-'ole out there: No, I said, *Where's this leadin' to? What's the 'ell-an'-glory use o' flushin' out this blarsted bit of a sink, with devil-knows-wot stinkin' cess-pool at the end of it!* That's wot I said, ma'am! . . .

AUNTIE. Very rightly! I see! I see! . . .

ROBERT. So up I go through the sludge, puffin' an' blowin' like a bally ole cart-'orse—strooth, it seemed miles! Talk abaht bee-utiful, ma'am, it ud 'a' done your 'eart good, it would really! *Rats!*— 'Undreds on em, ma'am: I'm bitten clean through in places! 'Owever, I pushed my way through, some-'ow, 'oldin' my nose an fightin' for my breath, till at last I got to the end—*and then I soon saw wot was the matter!* . . .

It's under the church—that's where it is! I know it's the church, cos I 'eard "The Church's One Foundation" on the orgin, rumblin' up over my 'ead! Well, I . . .

ALL. Yes . . . yes . . .

AUNTIE. Why don't you go on ? . . .

ROBERT. You'd never guess wot I saw there, not if you was to try from now till glory 'allelooyer!...

The biggest back-'ander, I ever did 'av', swelp me! . . .

[They hang on his words expectantly.]

It ain't no drain at all!

ALL [breathlessly]. Why, what is it, then? . . .

ROBERT. It's a grive!

ALL. A grave! . . .

ROBERT. Yus, one o' them whoppin' great beer-vaults as you shove big bugses' corpses inter! What d'yer think o' that now?

MARY. } Oh! . . .
AUNTIE. } Horrible! . . .

VICAR. I seem to remember some tradition . . .

ROBERT. You'd 'a' said so if you'd seen wot I seen! Talk abaht corfins an' shrouds an' bones an' dead men gone to rot, they wasn't in it, wot I saw dahn there! Madame Twosoes is a flea-bite to it! Lord!—I never thought there could be such a lot o' muck an' dead things all in one place before! It was a fair treat, it was, I tek my oath! . . .

[Rapturously]. Why—why, it may cost a man 'is LIFE to deal with that little job!

VICAR. My God! The thing's impossible!

ROBERT. Impossible! Means a bit of work, that's all!

VICAR. Why, no one would ever dare . . .

ROBERT. Dare! Why, wot d'you think I come 'ere for? . . .

VICAR. *You!* . . .

ROBERT. Yus—makin' myself unpleasant . . .

VICAR. Do you mean . . . Do I understand . . .

ROBERT. I mean as I've found *my place*, or I don't know a good thing when I see it!

AUNTIE. What! To go into that dreadful vault, and . . .

ROBERT. Why not: ain't it my job?

AUNTIE. But you said—perhaps—*death* . . .

ROBERT. It's worth it, it's a lovely bit of work!

VICAR. No, ten thousand times, no! The sacrifice is too much!

ROBERT. You call that sacrifice?—It's fun: not 'arf!

VICAR. I had rather see the church itself . . .

ROBERT. What, you call yourself a clergyman!

VICAR. I call myself nothing: I *am* nothing—less than nothing in all this living world!

ROBERT. By God, but I call myself summat—I'M THE DRAIN-MAN, THAT'S WOT I AM!

VICAR [feverishly]. You shall not go! . . .

ROBERT. Why, wot is there to fear? Ain't it worth while, to move away that load o' muck!

VICAR. The stench—the horror—the darkness . . .

ROBERT. What's it matter, if the comrides up above 'av' light an' joy an' a breath of 'olesome air to sing by? . . .

VICAR. Hour by hour—dying—alone . . .

ROBERT. The comrides up in the spans an arches, joinin' 'ands . . .

VICAR. Fainter and fainter, below there, and at last—an endless silence! . . .

ROBERT. 'Igh in the dome, the 'ammerin's of the comrides as 'av' climbed aloft!

AUNTIE. William, there is yet one other way! . . .

VICAR. Yes, yes, I see: I see! . . . [To ROBERT]. Then—you mean to go?

ROBERT. By 'Eaven, yus!

VICAR. Then, by God and all the powers of grace, you shall not go alone! Off with these lies and make-believes! Off with these prisoner's shackles! They cramp, they stifle me! Freedom! Freedom! This is no priest's work—it calls for a man! . . .

> [He tears off his parson's coat and
> collar, casting them furiously aside.
> He rolls up his sleeves.]

Now, if you're ready, Comrade: you and I to-gether!

AUNTIE. God's might go with you, William! Accept him, Christ!

> [There is a silence. Then ROBERT
> speaks with slow consideration.]

ROBERT. I—don't—know. It's dangerous, you understand!

VICAR. I go with you.

ROBERT. This ain't psalms an 'ymns an' ole maids' tea-parties, mind you! It may mean typhoid!

VICAR. I understand.

ROBERT. Rats.

VICAR. Yes.

ROBERT. They don't leave you alone: they got teeth, remember—poison in 'em!

VICAR. I will go with you.

> [A slight pause. Then ROBERT, dropping into a quite ordinary tone, says.]

ROBERT. Then let's 'av' summat to eat, an' get along. There's nuthin' more to say.

MARY [inspired]. Yes, there is!

ROBERT. What do you mean, miss?

MARY. I mean that I understand: that I know who you are.

ROBERT. Me? . . .

MARY [simply]. Yes, you are my father.

ROBERT. 'Ow the everlastin' did you know that?

MARY [going up to him]. Because you are my wish come true: because you are brave, because you are very beautiful, because you are good!

Robert. My little kid! My little kid!
> [They embrace each other.]

Vicar. Robert! [Taking his left hand].

Auntie. Brother! [Taking his other hand.]
> [They form a kind of cross.]
> [Manson and Rogers re-enter with table-cloth, etc., for lunch.]

Manson. Come along, Rogers. Take that end.
> [They lay the cloth, as it were with ceremonial gravity, Manson being at the upper end of the table. They pay no heed to the others, who watch them interestedly.]

Robert. I could just do with a good, square feed. My work meks me 'ungry.

Manson. Flowers, Rogers.
> [Rogers brings vase from sideboard and places it on the Vicar's side of the table. Manson removes it to a more communal position. Presently looking up, he sees the group to his left watching him.]

Oh, beg pardon, sir: perhaps you'd like to know —the Bishop of Benares is here.

Vicar. What, already! Let's have him in at once!

[MANSON deliberates with the flowers before he speaks.]

MANSON. He is here.

[The VICAR crosses towards him.]

VICAR. What do you mean? Where is he?

[MANSON looks at him over the flowers.]

MANSON. Here.

[The VICAR steps back, gazing at
him. After a moment he gasps.]

VICAR. In God's name, who are you?

MANSON. In God's Name—your brother.

[He holds out his hand. The VICAR
takes it, sinking to his knees and
sobbing as one broken yet healed.]
[The curtain descends slowly.]

THE END